SIDE BY SIDE
English Grammar
Through
Guided Conversations
BOOK ONE

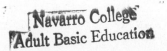

SIDE BY SIDE

English Grammar Through Guided Conversations

BOOK ONE

Steven J. Molinsky

Bill Bliss

Illustrated by

Richard E. Hill

Prentice-Hall Inc., Englewood Cliffs, New Jersey 07632

Library of Congress Cataloging in Publication Data

MOLINSKY, STEVEN J
    Side by Side

        Includes index
            1. English language—Conversation and phrase books.
    2. English language—Text-books for foreigners.
    I. BLISS, BILL, joint author.   II. Title.
    PE1131.M58   428'.3'4   79-19946
    ISBN 0-13-809848-4 (v. 1)

Printed in the United States of America

19   18   17   16

Editorial/production supervisor: Penelope Linskey
Art/camera copy supervisor: Diane Heckler-Koromhas
Cover design by Suzanne Behnke
Manufacturing buyer: Harry P. Baisley

PRENTICE-HALL INTERNATIONAL, INC., *London*
PRENTICE-HALL OF AUSTRALIA PTY. LIMITED, *Sydney*
PRENTICE-HALL OF CANADA, LTD., *Toronto*
PRENTICE-HALL OF INDIA PRIVATE LIMITED, *New Delhi*
PRENTICE-HALL OF JAPAN, INC., *Tokyo*
PRENTICE-HALL OF SOUTHEAST ASIA PTE. LTD., *Singapore*
WHITEHALL BOOKS LIMITED, WELLINGTON, *New Zealand*

Contents

To the Teacher

Side by Side is a conversational grammar book.

We do not seek to describe the language, or prescribe its rules. Rather, we aim to help students learn to *use* the language grammatically, through practice with meaningful conversational exchanges.

This book is intended for adult and young-adult learners of English. It is designed to provide the beginning student with the basic foundation of English grammar, through a carefully sequenced progression of conversational exercises and activities. Teachers of nonbeginning students will also find these materials to be effective as a rapid, concise review of basic structures of the language.

WHY A CONVERSATIONAL GRAMMAR BOOK?

Grammar is usually isolated and drilled through a variety of traditional structural exercises such as repetition, substitution, and transformation drills. These exercises effectively highlight particular grammatical structures . . . but they are usually presented as a string of single sentences, not related to each other in any unifying, relevant context.

Traditional dialogues, on the other hand, may do a fine job of providing examples of real speech, but they don't usually offer sufficient practice with the structures being taught. Teachers and students are often frustrated by the lack of a clear grammatical focus in these meaningful contexts. And besides that, it's hard to figure out what to *do* with a dialogue after you've read it, memorized it, or talked about it.

In this book we have attempted to combine the best features of traditional grammatical drills and contextually rich dialogues. We aim to actively engage our students in meaningful conversational exchanges within carefully structured grammatical frameworks. And we encourage our students to then break away from the textbook and *use* these frameworks to create conversations *on their own*.

While we have designed this text for the beginning student, we are also concerned about the nonbeginner. Although this student has made progress in understanding and using the language, he or she often needs more practice with the basics, the "nuts and bolts" of elementary English grammar.

(Intermediate-level teachers often tell us that even though their students are doing beautifully with the present perfect tense, they still have trouble with such "early" structures as the third-person singular -s or the difference between the simple present and present continuous tenses.)

This book offers nonbeginners the opportunity to use their richer vocabularies in open-ended conversational exercises which focus on the basic grammatical structures of the language.

AN OVERVIEW

GRAMMATICAL PARADIGMS

Each lesson in the book covers one or more specific grammatical structures. A new structure appears first in the form of a grammatical paradigm, a simple schema of the structure.

These paradigms are meant to be a reference point for students as they proceed through the lesson's conversational activities. While these paradigms highlight the structures being taught, we don't intend them to be goals in themselves.

We don't want our students simply to parrot back these rules: we want them to engage in conversations that show they can *use* them correctly.

GUIDED CONVERSATIONS

Guided conversations are the dialogues and the question and answer exchanges which are the primary learning devices in this book. Students are presented with a model conversation that highlights a specific aspect of the grammar. In the exercises that follow the model, students pair up and work "Side by Side," placing new content into the given conversational framework.

How to Introduce Guided Conversations

There are many alternative ways to introduce these conversations. We don't want to dictate any particular method. Rather, we encourage you to develop strategies that are compatible with your own teaching style, the specific needs of your students, and the particular grammar and content of the lesson at hand.

Some teachers will want books closed at this stage, so their students will have a chance to listen to the model before seeing it in print.

Other teachers will want students to have their books open for the model conversation or see it written on the blackboard. The teacher may read or act out the conversation while students follow along, or may read through the model with another student, or may have two students present the model to the class.

Whether books are open or closed, students should have ample opportunity to understand and practice the model before attempting the exercises that follow it.

How to Use Guided Conversations

In these conversational exercises, we are asking our students to place new content into the grammatical and contextual framework of the model. The numbered exercises provide the student with new information which is "plugged into" the framework of the model conversation. Sometimes this framework actually appears as a "skeletal dialogue" in the text. Other times the student simply inserts the new information into the model that has just been practiced. (Teachers who have written the model conversation on the blackboard can create the skeletal dialogue by erasing the words that are replaced in the exercises.)

The teacher's key function is to pair up students for "Side by Side" conversational practice, and then to serve as a resource to the class, for help with the structure, new vocabulary, and pronunciation.

"Side by Side" practice can take many forms. Most teachers prefer to call on two students at a time to present a conversation to the class. Other teachers have all their students pair up and practice the conversations with a partner. Or small groups of students might work together, pairing up within these groups and presenting the conversations to others in the group.

This paired practice helps teachers address the varying levels of ability of their students. Some teachers like to pair stronger students with weaker ones. The slower student clearly gains through this pairing, while the more advanced student also strengthens his or her abilities by lending assistance to the speaking partner.

Other teachers will want to pair up or group students of *similar* levels of ability. In this arrangement, the teacher can devote greater attention to students who need it, while giving more capable students the chance to learn from and assist each other.

While these exercises are intended for practice in conversation, teachers also find them useful as *writing* drills which reinforce oral practice and enable students to study more carefully the grammar highlighted in these conversations.

Once again, we encourage you to develop strategies that are most appropriate for your class.

The "Life Cycle" of a Guided Conversation

It might be helpful to define the different stages in the "life cycle" of a guided conversation.

1. *The Presentation Stage*
   The model conversation is introduced and practiced by the class.

2. *The Rehearsal Stage*
   Immediately after practicing the model, students do the conversational exercises that follow. For homework, they practice these conversations, and perhaps write out a few. Some lessons also ask students to create their own original conversations based on the model.

3. *The Performance Stage*
   The next day students do the conversational exercises in class, preferably with their textbooks and notebooks closed. Students shouldn't have to memorize these conversations. They will most likely remember them after sufficient practice in class and at home.

4. *The Incorporation Stage*
   The class reviews the conversation or pieces of the conversation in the days that follow. With repetition and time, the guided conversation "dissolves" and its components are incorporated into the student's active language.

ON YOUR OWN

An important component of each lesson is the "On Your Own" activity. These student-centered exercises reinforce the grammatical structures of the lesson while breaking away from the text and allowing students to contribute content of their own.

These activities take various forms: role-plays, interviews, extended guided conversations, and questions about the student's real world.

In these exercises, we ask students to bring to the classroom new content, based on their interests, their backgrounds, and the farthest reaches of their imaginations.

We recommend that the teacher read through these activities in class and assign them as homework for presentation the next day. In this way, students will automatically review the previous day's grammar while contributing new and inventive content of their own.

"On Your Own" activities are meant for simultaneous grammar reinforcement and vocabulary building. Beginning students will tend to recycle previous textbook vocabulary into these activities. While this repetition is clearly useful, beginners should also be encouraged to use other words which are familiar to them but are not in the text. *All* students should be encouraged to use a dictionary in completing the "On Your Own" activities. In this way, they will not only use the words they know, but the words they would *like* to know in order to really bring their interests, backgrounds, and imaginations into the classroom.

As a result, students will be teaching each other new vocabulary and also sharing a bit of their lives with others in the class.

CLASSROOM DRAMAS

"Classroom Dramas" are the full-page comic strip dialogues that appear every once in a while throughout the text. The goal of these dialogues is to tackle a specific grammatical structure and give students the opportunity to rehearse this structure in a short, playful classroom conversation.

Some teachers will simply want to read through these dramas with their students. Others might want to act them out, using students in the class as the characters.

Students enjoy memorizing these dramas and using them frequently throughout the course. In fact, they often break into these conversations spontaneously, without any prompting from the teacher. (Our students, for example, like to impress visitors to the class by confidently performing these dramas as though they were really happening for the first time.)

In conclusion, we have attempted to make the study of English grammar a lively and relevant experience for our students. While we hope that we have conveyed to you the substance of our textbook, we also hope that we have conveyed the spirit: that learning the grammar can be conversational . . . student-centered . . . and fun.

Steven J. Molinsky
Bill Bliss

SIDE BY SIDE

English Grammar
Through
Guided Conversations

BOOK ONE

To Be: Introduction

Read and practice.

Answer these questions.

1. What is your name?

   _____

2. What is your address?

   _____

3. What is your phone number?

   _____

4. Where are you from?

   _____

Now ask the other students in your class.

*Pronounce: two thirty-five.
†Pronounce: seven four one, eight nine "oh" six. (For the complete list of numbers, see page 198.)

Interview a famous person. Make up addresses, phone numbers, and cities. Use your imagination. Role-play these interviews in class.

A. What is your name?

B. My name is _____.

A. _____ address?

B. _____.

A. _____ phone number?

B. _____.

A. Where are you from?

B. _____.

A. Thank you very much.

B. You're welcome.

a famous actor

a famous actress

a famous athlete

*the president/prime minister
of your country*

To Be + Location
Subject Pronouns

bedroom

bathroom

garage

living room

dining room

kitchen

yard

basement

I	am	I'm	
He She It	is →	He's She's It's	in the kitchen.
We You They	are	We're You're They're	

	am	I
Where	is	he she it
	are	we you they	?

Read and practice.

Answer these questions.

1. Where are you?

2. Where are you?

3. Where are you?

4. Where are you?

5. Where are Bill and Mary?

6. Where are Mr. and Mrs. Wilson?

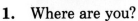

7. Where are you?

8. Where are you and Tom?

9. Where are Mr. and Mrs. Johnson?

Read and practice.

*Where is → Where's

Answer these questions.

1. Where's Tom?

2. Where's Fred?

3. Where's Helen?

4. Where's Betty?

5. Where's the newspaper?

6. Where's the cat?

7. Where's Jane?

8. Where's John?

9. Where's the dog?

WHERE ARE THEY?

Ask and answer questions based on these pictures.

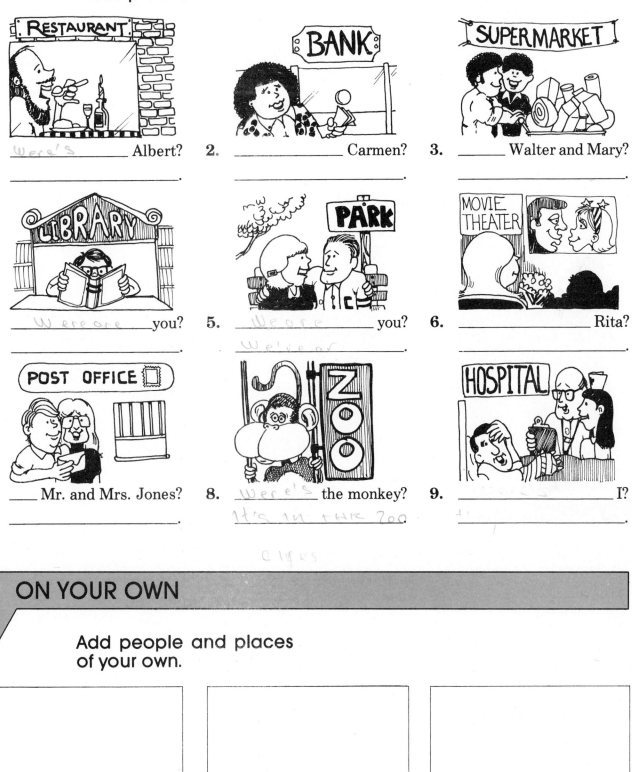

1. _Were's_ _____ Albert?

_____.

2. _____ Carmen?

3. _____ Walter and Mary?

4. _W ere are_ _____ you?

_____.

5. _We are_ _____ you?

_We'ie ar_

6. _____ Rita?

7. _____ Mr. and Mrs. Jones?

_____.

8. _Were's_ ____ the monkey?

It's in the zoo.

clges

9. _____ I?

_____.

ON YOUR OWN

Add people and places of your own.

10. _____ ?

_____.

11. _____ ?

_____.

12. _____ ?

_____.

Present Continuous Tense

I	am	
He		
She	is	
It		eating.
We		
You	are	
They		

am	I		
	is	he	
What		she	
		it	doing?
	are	we	
		you	
		they	

Read and practice.

*What is → what's.

Complete these conversations.

1. What are you doing?
   _____I'm_____ reading the newspaper.

2. _____ Mr. and Mrs. Jones doing?
   _____their_____ eating dinner.

3. __Wh_____ Henry doing?
   __He is_____ cooking dinner.

4. _____ Maria doing?
   _____ studying English.

5. _____ Frank doing?
   _____ sleeping.

6. __What are__ Sam and Betty doing?
   _____ watching TV.

7. __what are_____ Judy doing?
   _____ playing the piano.

8. What are YOU doing?
   I'm _____.

WHERE ARE THEY AND WHAT ARE THEY DOING?

Ask and answer these questions.

1. Where's Walter?
   He's in the kitchen.
   What's he doing?
   He's eating breakfast.

2. _____Where's_____ Betty?
   _____She's in the_____ park.
   _____What's   She_____ doing?
   _____She's eati_____ eating lunch.

3. _____Where's_____ Mr. and Mrs. Smith?
   _____they're in the_____ dining room.
   _____what's   they_____ doing?
   _____they're   eati_____ eating dinner.

4. _____Where are_____ you?
   _____I'm in the_____ bedroom.
   _____ doing?
   _____ playing the guitar.

5. _____ you?
   _____ living room.
   _____ doing?
   _____ playing cards.

6. _____where are_____ Tom and Mary?
   _____ yard.
   _____ doing?
   _____ playing baseball.

7. _____ Miss Jackson?
   _____ restaurant.
   _____ doing?
   _____ drinking coffee.

8. _____ Mr. Larson?
   _____ cafeteria.
   _____ doing?
   _____ drinking lemonade.

9. _____ you?

_____ library.

_____ doing?

_____ studying English.

10. _____ Tommy?

_____ classroom.

_____ doing?

_____ studying mathematics.

11. _____ Gloria?

_____ discotheque.

_____ doing?

_____ dancing.

12. _____ Harry?

_____ bathroom.

_____ doing?

_____ singing.

13. _____ Barbara?

_____ hospital.

_____ doing?

_____ watching TV.

14. _____ you?

_____ park.

_____ doing?

_____ listening to the radio.

ON YOUR OWN

Add people, places, and actions of your own.

15. _____?

_____.

_____?

_____.

16. _____?

_____.

_____?

_____.

To Be: Short Answers
Possessive Adjectives

I	my
he	his
she	her
it	its
we	our
you	your
they	their

Read and practice.

we (our)

	I	am.
Yes,	{ he she it }	is.
	{ we you they }	are.

Read and practice.

Complete these conversations using the model above.

1. Is Nancy busy?
washing her car

2. Is Ted busy?
feeding his dog

3. Are you busy?
cleaning our yard

4. Are Mr. and Mrs. Jones busy?
painting their kitchen

yes

5. Are you busy?
doing my homework

6. Is Peter busy?
doing his exercises

yes he

7. Is Linda busy?
fixing her bicycle

8. Are you busy?
cleaning our apartment

9. Are Bob and Judy busy?
washing their windows

10. Is Michael busy?
feeding his cat

11. Are you busy?
washing my clothes

12. Are you busy?
fixing our TV

13. Is Henry busy?
cleaning his garage

14. Are your children busy?
brushing their teeth

Use this model to talk about the picture above with other students in your class.

A. Where's Miss Johnson?

B. She's in the parking lot.

A. What's she doing?

B. She's washing her car.

To Be:
Yes/No Questions
Short Answers
Adjectives
Possessive Nouns

I	am	
He		
She	is	
It		tall.
We		
You	are	
They		

Read and practice.

Bob — *tall*   **Bill** — *short*

A. Is Bob tall or short?

B. He's tall.

A. Is Bill tall or short?

B. He's short.

Answer these questions.

Alice — *young*   Margaret — *old*

1. Is Alice young or old?

2. Is Margaret young or old?

Herman — *heavy fat*   David — *thin*

3. Is Herman heavy or thin?

4. Is David fat or thin?

Herman's car — *new*   David's car — *old*

5. Is Herman's car new or old?

6. Is David's car new or old?

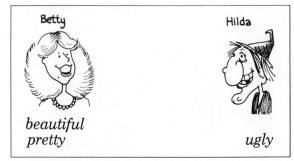

Betty — *beautiful pretty*   Hilda — *ugly*

7. Is Betty beautiful or ugly?

8. Is Hilda pretty or ugly?

9. Is Edward handsome or ugly?

10. Is Captain Blood handsome or ugly?

11. Is Albert rich or poor?

12. Is John rich or poor?

13. Is Albert's house large or small?

14. Is John's apartment big or little?

15. Are Mary's neighbors noisy or quiet?

16. Are Jane's neighbors loud or quiet?

17. Is champagne expensive or cheap?

18. Is tea expensive or cheap?

19. Is Barbara married or single?

20. Is Julie married or single?

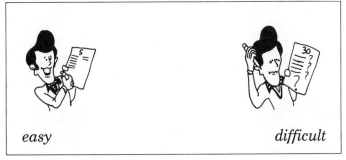

21. Are the questions in Chapter 5 easy or difficult?

22. Are the questions in Chapter 30 easy or difficult?

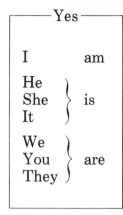
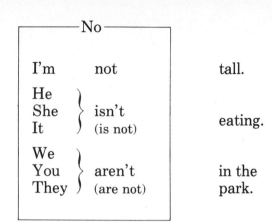

?		Yes		No	
Am	I	I	am	I'm	not	tall.
Is	{ he she it	He She It	} is	He She It	} isn't (is not)	eating.
Are	{ we you they	We You They	} are	We You They	} aren't (are not)	in the park.

Read and practice.

Are you married?

No, I'm not. I'm single.

Tell me about your new car. Is it large?

No, it isn't. It's small.

Tell me about your new neighbors. Are they quiet?

No, they aren't. They're noisy.

Answer these questions.

1. Tell me about your brother.

_____ _____ tall?

No, _____.

2. Tell me about your sister.

_____ _____ single?

No, _____.

3. Tell me about your apartment.

_____ _____ new?

No, _____.

4. Tell me about your new boss.

_____ _____ old?

No, _____.

5. Tell me about Stanley's Restaurant.

_____ _____ expensive?

No, _____.

6. Tell me about your neighbors.

_____ _____ noisy?

No, _____.

7. Tell me about Henry's cat.

_____ _____ pretty?

No, _____.

8. Tell me about Fred and Sally's dog.

_____ _____ little?

No, _____.

9. Tell me about the questions in your English book.

_____ _____ difficult?

No, _____.

10. Tell me about Santa Claus.

_____ _____ thin?

No, _____.

THE WEATHER

It's sunny.

It's cloudy.

It's raining.

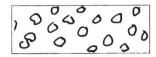
It's snowing.

It's hot.

It's warm.

It's cool.

It's cold.

How's the weather today in YOUR city?

ON YOUR OWN

Read and practice.

A LONG-DISTANCE TELEPHONE CALL

A. Hi, Jack. This is Jim. I'm calling from Miami.

B. From Miami? What are you doing in Miami?

A. I'm on vacation.

B. How's the weather in Miami? Is it sunny?

A. No, it isn't. It's cloudy.

B. Is it hot?

A. No, it isn't. It's cold.

B. Are you having a good time?

A. No, I'm not. I'm having a TERRIBLE time. The weather is TERRIBLE here.

B. I'm sorry to hear that.

A. Hi, _____. This is _____. I'm calling from _____.

B. From _____? What are you doing in _____?

A. I'm on vacation.

B. How's the weather in _____? Is it _____?

A. No, it isn't. It's _____.

B. Is it _____?

A. No, it isn't. It's _____.

B. Are you having a good time?

A. No, I'm not. I'm having a TERRIBLE time. The weather is TERRIBLE here.

B. I'm sorry to hear that.

You're on vacation and the weather is terrible. Call a student in your class. Use the conversation above as a guide.

1. *Switzerland*
cool?
snowing?

2. *Honolulu*
hot?
sunny?

3. _____

	I	am.
Yes,	he she it	is.
	we you they	are.

	I'm not.	
No,	he she it	isn't.
	we you they	aren't.

Act this out in class.

YOU'RE A GENIUS!

To Be: Review

Read and practice.

MY FAVORITE PHOTOGRAPHS

A. Who is he?

B. He's my father.

A. What's his name?

B. His name is Paul.

A. Where is he (in this photograph)?

B. He's in Paris.

A. What's he doing?

B. He's standing in front of the Eiffel Tower.

Using these questions, talk about the photographs below.

Who is he/she? (Who are they?)

What _____ name (names)?

Where _____?

What _____ doing?

1. *my wife*
in New York
standing in front of the
  Statue of Liberty

2. *my son*
in the park
playing soccer

3. *my daughter*
in her bedroom
sleeping

4. *my brother*
at the beach
swimming

5. *my sister and her husband*
at our house
standing in front of the fireplace

6. *my mother*
in our living room
sitting on the sofa and
watching TV

7. *my aunt and uncle*
in their dining room
having dinner

8. *my cousin*
in front of his house
washing his car

9. *my grandmother and grandfather*
at my wedding
crying

10. *my cousin*
in the park
sitting on a bench and
feeding the birds

11. *my friend*
sitting on his bed
playing the guitar

12. *my wife's brother**
in Washington
standing in front of the
Washington Monument

13. *my brother's wife†*
in their apartment
painting their living room

14. *my friends*
at my birthday party
singing and dancing

*Or: my brother-in-law.
† Or: my sister-in-law.

ON YOUR OWN

Bring in your favorite photographs.
Talk about them with other students
in your class. Ask the other students
about their favorite photographs.

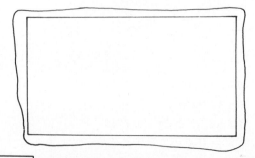

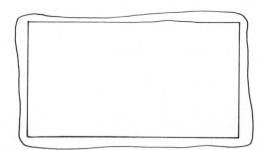

Prepositions
There Is/There Are
Singular/Plural:
Introduction

Read and practice.

Where's the restaurant?
It's **next to** the bank.

Where's the school?
It's **between** the library and the park.

Where's the supermarket?
It's **across from** the movie theater.

Where's the post office?
It's **around the corner from** the hospital.

1. Where's the park?

2. Where's the bank?

3. Where's the church?

4. Where's the movie theater?

5. Where's the restaurant?

6. Where's the police station?

7. Where's the fire station?

8. Where's the post office?

> **There's (there is)** a bank on Main Street.
> **Is there** a bank on Main Street?

Read and practice.

A. Excuse me. Is there a laundromat in this neighborhood?*

B. Yes, there is. There's a laundromat on Main Street, next to the supermarket.

*You can say "in this neighborhood" or "nearby."

1. *post office?*

2. *bank?*

3. *movie theater?*

4. *gas station?*

5. *bus station?*

6. *cafeteria?*

7. *drugstore?*

8. *library?*

| Is there . . . ? | Yes, there is. |
| | No, there isn't. |

Read and practice.

WHAT'S IN YOUR NEIGHBORHOOD?

Draw a simple map of your neighborhood. Pair off with another student in the class and ask each other about your neighborhoods. Here are some places you might want to include in your questions.

bakery	church	gas station	police station
bank	clinic	hospital	post office
barber shop	department store	laundromat	restaurant
beauty parlor	doctor's office	library	school
bus station	drugstore	movie theater	supermarket
cafeteria	fire station	park	train station

Singular		Plural	
a student a room an exercise	Yes, there is. No, there isn't.	students rooms exercises	Yes, there are. No, there aren't.

ON YOUR OWN

LOOKING FOR AN APARTMENT

You're looking for a new apartment. Another student in your class is the landlord. Ask the landlord about the apartment on page 39.

1. Is there a stove in the kitchen?
2. Is there a refrigerator in the kitchen?
3. Is there a superintendent in the building?
4. Is there an elevator in the building?
5. Is there a fire escape?
6. Is there a TV antenna on the roof?
7. Is there a radiator in every room?
8. Is there a mailbox near the building?
9. Is there a bus stop near the building?
10. Are there any pets in the building?
11. Are there any children in the building?
12. How many rooms are there in the apartment? (There are four rooms in the apartment.)
13. How many floors are there in the building?
14. How many closets are there in the bedroom?
15. How many windows are there in the living room?

Ask the landlord some other questions.

_____

_____

_____

Are there any problems in the apartment on page 39? Don't ask the landlord! Another student in your class is a tenant in the building. Ask that student.

16. Are there any mice in the basement?
17. Are there any cockroaches in the apartment?
18. Are there any broken windows?
19. Are there any holes in the walls?

Ask the tenant some other questions.

_____

_____

_____

Singular/Plural
This/That/These/Those

Say these words after your teacher
and then place them in the chart
on the next page.

hat
glasses
shirt
tie
jacket
watch
belt
pants
sock
shoe

earring
necklace
blouse
bracelet
skirt
stocking

coat
glove
pocketbook
dress

suit
raincoat
umbrella
briefcase

sweater
mitten
boot

Singular/Plural*

[s]	[z]	[iz]
a book – books	a car – cars	a class – classes
a shop – shops	a school – schools	a church – churches
a student – students	a window – windows	a garage – garages
a bank – banks	a store – stores	an exercise – exercises
an airport – airports	an island – islands	an office – offices

a hat – hats

---

*Some words have irregular plurals:

man – men
woman – women
child – children
person – people
tooth – teeth
mouse – mice

Colors

red   orange   yellow   green   blue   purple   black   brown

pink   gray   white   gold   silver

Read and practice.

IN THE DEPARTMENT STORE

A. May I help you?

B. Yes, please. I'm looking for a jacket.

A. Here's a nice jacket.

B. But this jacket is PURPLE!

A. That's O.K.* Purple jackets are very POPULAR this year.

*This is sometimes spelled: okay.

A. May I help you?

B. Yes, please. I'm looking for a _____.

A. Here's a nice _____.

B. But this _____ is _____!

A. That's O.K. _____ _____s are very POPULAR this year.

1. *green!*

2. *orange!*

3. *red!*

4. *yellow!*

5. *purple!*

6. *pink and green!*

7. *polka dot!*

8. *striped!*

Read and practice.

A. May I help you?

B. Yes, please. I'm looking for a pair of gloves.

A. Here's a nice pair of gloves.

B. But these gloves are GREEN!

A. That's O.K. Green gloves are very POPULAR this year.

A. May I help you?

B. Yes, please. I'm looking for a pair of _____.

A. Here's a nice pair of _____.

B. But these _____ are _____!

A. That's O.K. _____ _____s are very POPULAR this year.

1. *pink!*   2. *black!*   3. *red!*   4. *striped!*

5. *green and yellow!*   6. *purple and brown!*   7. *polka dot!*   8. *red, white, and blue!*

Talk about colors with the students in your class.

What are you wearing today?
What are the students in your class wearing today?
What's your favorite color?

Read and practice.

1. *pen*

2. *book*

3. *pencils*

4. *mittens*

5. *raincoat*

6. *earrings*

7. *sweater*

8. *boots*

Practice these conversations.

LOST AND FOUND

A. Is THIS your umbrella?

B. No, it isn't.

A. Are you sure?

B. Yes, I'm sure.
THAT umbrella is brown, and MY umbrella is black.

A. Are THESE your boots?

B. No, they aren't.

A. Are you sure?

B. Yes, I'm sure.
THOSE boots are dirty, and MY boots are clean.

Make up conversations, using colors and other adjectives you know.

1. *watch*

2. *glasses*

3. *pocketbook*

4. *gloves*

5. *little boy*

6. _____

Act this out, using names of students
in your class.

This/That

Act this out, using names of students
in your class.

These/Those

Simple Present Tense

| $\left.\begin{array}{l}\text{I}\\\text{We}\\\text{You}\\\text{They}\end{array}\right\}$ live. | Where do $\left.\begin{array}{l}\text{I}\\\text{we}\\\text{you}\\\text{they}\end{array}\right\}$ live? | What do $\left.\begin{array}{l}\text{I}\\\text{we}\\\text{you}\\\text{they}\end{array}\right\}$ do? |

Read and practice.

Hello! My name is Antonio.
I live in Rome.
I speak Italian.

Every day

I eat Italian food,
I drink Italian wine,*
and I sing Italian songs.

I think Rome is a wonderful city.
I'm glad I live here.

*In practicing, you can say: coffee, tea, beer, etc.

INTERVIEWS AROUND THE WORLD

Interview these people, using the questions below.

What's your name?
Where do you live?
What language do you speak?
What do you do every day?

1. French — Marie (PARIS)
2. Spanish — Carlos (MADRID)
3. German — Frieda (BERLIN)
4. Japanese — Toshi (TOKYO)
5. English — Sara and Mark (LONDON)
6. Russian — Boris and Natasha (MOSCOW)

He She } lives. It	Where does { he she } live? it	What does { he she } do? it

Read and practice.

A. What's his name?

B. His name is Miguel.

A. Where does he live?

B. He lives in Mexico City.

A. What language does he speak?

B. He speaks Spanish.

A. What does he do every day?

B. He eats Mexican food,
he reads Mexican newspapers,
and he listens to Mexican music.

Ask and answer questions about these people.

What's his/her name?
Where does he/she live?
What language does he/she speak?
What does he/she do every day?

1.

2.

Margarita

3.

4.

5.

6.

| I We You They | } live. |
| He She It | } lives. |

| Where | do | I we you they | } | live? |
| | does | he she it | } | |

| What | do | I we you they | } | do? |
| | does | he she it | } | |

ON YOUR OWN

Interview a famous person.

A. What's your name?

B. _____.

A. _____ live?

B. _____.

A. _____ speak?

B. _____.

A. _____ every day?

B. _____.

Now tell the class about this person.

His/Her name is _____

_____

_____

_____

Simple Present Tense:
Yes/No Questions
Negatives
Short Answers

He cooks. He doesn't cook. (does not)	Does he cook? Yes, he does. No, he doesn't.	When What kind of food } does he cook?

STANLEY'S INTERNATIONAL RESTAURANT

Stanley's International Restaurant is a very special place.
Every day Stanley cooks a different kind of food.

Italian MONDAY	Greek TUESDAY	Chinese WEDNESDAY	Puerto Rican THURSDAY	Japanese FRIDAY	Mexican SATURDAY	American SUNDAY

What kind of food does Stanley cook on Monday?
   On Monday he cooks Italian food.

What kind of food does he cook on Tuesday? on Wednesday?
on Thursday? on Friday? on Saturday? on Sunday?

A. Does Stanley cook Greek food on Tuesday?

B. Yes, he does.

Ask five questions with "yes" answers.

A. Does Stanley cook Japanese food on Sunday?

B. No, he doesn't.

A. When does he cook Japanese food?

B. He cooks Japanese food on Friday.

Ask five questions with "no" answers.

You go. You don't go. (do not)	Do you go? Yes, I do. No, I don't.	When do you go?

A. Do you go to Stanley's International Restaurant on Wednesday?
B. Yes, I do.
A. Why?
B. Because I like Chinese food.

Ask these people.

1. *Friday*
Japanese

2. *Saturday*
Mexican

3. *Monday*
Italian

4. *Thursday*
Puerto Rican

A. Do you go to Stanley's International Restaurant on Sunday?
B. No, I don't.
A. Why not?
B. Because I don't like American food.

Ask these people.

5. *Monday*
Italian

6. *Tuesday*
Greek

7. *Wednesday*
Chinese

8. *Saturday*
Mexican

A. What kind of food do you like?
B. I like Russian food.
A. When do you go to Stanley's International Restaurant?
B. I don't go to Stanley's International Restaurant.
A. Why not?
B. Because Stanley doesn't cook Russian food.

Ask these people.

9. *French*

10. *German*

11. *Arabic*

12. *Hungarian*

What do people do at Stanley's International Restaurant?

On Monday they speak Italian, eat Italian food, drink Italian wine, smoke Italian cigarettes, and listen to Italian music.

1.

Henry likes Greek food.

When does he go to Stanley's International Restaurant?

What does he do there?

2.

Mr. and Mrs. Wilson go to Stanley's International Restaurant on Wednesday.

What kind of food do they like?

What do they do there?

Ask another student in your class.

When do you go to Stanley's International Restaurant?

Why?

What do you do there?

Answer these questions and then ask another student in your class.

1. **a.** What kind of movies do you like? (Do you like comedies? dramas? westerns? war movies? science fiction? cartoons?)

   b. Who is your favorite movie actor? actress?

2. **a.** What kind of books do you like? (Do you like novels? poetry? short stories?)

   b. Who is your favorite author?

3. What school subjects do you like? (Do you like English? science? history? mathematics?)

4. **a.** What kind of TV programs do you like? (Do you like comedies? dramas? westerns? cartoons?)

   b. Who is your favorite TV star?

5. What's your favorite food?

6. **a.** What kind of music do you like? (Do you like classical music? popular music? jazz? rock and roll?)

   b. Who is your favorite singer? (What kind of songs does he/she sing?)

7. **a.** Which sports do you like? (Do you like football? baseball? soccer? golf? hockey? tennis?)

   b. Who is your favorite athlete?

Yes, { I / we / you / they } do.

{ he / she / it } does.

No, { I / we / you / they } don't.

{ he / she / it } doesn't.

Act this out in class.

YOU SPEAK ENGLISH VERY WELL

Object Pronouns
Simple Present Tense:
s vs. non-s endings
Adverbs of Frequency

I	me
he	him
she	her
it	it
we	us
you	you
they	them

Read and practice.

FRIENDS

Do you like me?

Of course I like you. You're my friend.

1.
Do you like John?
Of course I like him. He's my friend.

2.
Does John like you?
Of course he likes me. I'm his friend.

3.
Do you like Mary?
Of course I like her. She's my friend.

4.
Does Mary like you?
Of course she likes me. I'm her friend.

5.
Do you like Bob and Betty?
Of course I like them. They're my friends.

6.
Do Bob and Betty like you?
Of course they like me. I'm their friend.

7.
Do you like Bob and Betty?
Of course we like them. They're our friends.

8.
Do Bob and Betty like you?
Of course they like us. We're their friends.

Now try this using the names of students in your class.

[s]	[z]	[iz]	
sit sits help helps look looks think thinks talk talks	read reads feed feeds love loves go goes	watch watches dance dances wash washes fix fixes	always 100% usually 90% sometimes 50% rarely 10% never 0%

Read and practice.

HARRY!   I'M REALLY UPSET!

1. When we sit in the living room, you always watch TV and never look at me.
2. When we eat breakfast together, you always read the newspaper and never talk to me.
3. When we go to parties, you usually sit with your friends and rarely dance with me.
4. And you're lazy! You never help me.
5. When our windows are dirty, you never wash them.
6. When our car is broken, you never fix it.
7. And when our cats are hungry, you never feed them.
8. Sometimes I think you don't love me.

WHY IS SHE UPSET WITH HARRY?

1. When they sit in the living room he always _____.
2. _____.
3. _____.
4. _____.
5. _____.
6. _____.
7. _____.
8. _____.

I We You They $\Big\}$ have	He She It $\Big\}$ has

Read and practice.

DO YOU LOOK LIKE YOUR BROTHER?

My brother and I look very different.

I have brown eyes and he has blue eyes.
We both have brown hair, but I have short,
curly hair and he has long, straight hair.
I'm tall and thin. He's short and heavy.

No, I don't look like my brother. We look very different.

ON YOUR OWN

Answer these questions.

1. **Who Do You Look Like?**

   I look like _____.

   We're both _____.
   We both have _____.

2. **Who DON'T You Look Like?**

   I don't look like _____.

   _____.

   _____.

   _____.

Read and practice.

MY SISTER AND I ARE VERY DIFFERENT

My sister and I are very different.

    I'm a teacher. She's a journalist.
    I live in Chicago. She lives in Paris.
    I have a small house in the suburbs. She has a large apartment in the city.
    I'm married. She's single.
    I play golf. She plays tennis.
    I play the piano. She doesn't play a musical instrument.
    On the weekend I usually watch TV and rarely go out. She never watches TV and always goes to parties.

We're very different. But we're sisters . . . and we're friends.

ON YOUR OWN

Compare yourself with a member of your family, another student in the class, or a famous person.

_____ and I Are Very Different

		I	He/She
a.	(occupation?)	I _____	He/She _____
b.	(city?)	_____	_____
c.	(house? apartment?)	_____	_____
d.	(single? married? divorced?)	_____	_____
e.	(play a sport?)	_____	_____
f.	(play an instrument?)	_____	_____
g.	(on the weekend?)	_____	_____

Contrast:
Simple Present and
Present Continuous Tenses

Why Are You Crying?

I'm crying because I'm sad.
I ALWAYS cry when I'm sad.

1. Why are you smiling?

_____ happy.

I ALWAYS _____.

2. Why is he shouting?

_____ angry.

He ALWAYS _____.

3. Why is she smoking?

_____ nervous.

She ALWAYS _____.

4. Why is it drinking?

_____ thirsty.

It ALWAYS _____.

5. Why are they going to
Stanley's Restaurant?

_____ hungry.

They ALWAYS _____.

6. Why is he going to the
doctor?

_____ sick.

He ALWAYS _____.

7. Why are they shivering?

_____ cold.

They ALWAYS _____.

8. Why are you perspiring?

_____ hot.

I ALWAYS _____.

9. Why is she yawning?

_____ tired.

She ALWAYS _____.

10. Why is he blushing?

_____ embarrassed.

He ALWAYS _____.

What do you do when you're nervous?

Do you smoke?

Do you perspire?

Do you bite your nails?

Answer these questions and then ask another student in your class.

What do you do when you're . . .

1. nervous?

When I'm nervous I bite my nails.

2. sad?

3. happy?

4. tired?

5. sick?

6. cold?

7. hot?

8. hungry?

9. thirsty?

10. angry?

11. embarrassed?

Read and practice this conversation.

A. What are you doing?!

B. I'm washing the dishes in the bathtub.

A. That's strange! Do you USUALLY wash the dishes in the bathtub?

B. No. I NEVER wash the dishes in the bathtub, but I'm washing the dishes in the bathtub TODAY.

A. Why are you washing the dishes in the bathtub?

B. Because my SINK is broken.

A. I'm sorry to hear that.

A. What are you doing?!

B. I'm _____.

A. That's strange! Do you USUALLY _____?

B. No, I NEVER _____, but I'm _____ TODAY.

A. Why are you _____?

B. Because my _____ is broken.

A. I'm sorry to hear that.

1. *sleep*
sleeping } *on the floor*
bed

2. *cook*
cooking } *on the radiator*
stove

3. *study*
studying } *English by candlelight*
lamp

4. *shout*
shouting } *to my neighbor across*
the street

telephone

5. *hitchhike*
hitchhiking } *to work*
car

6.

13

**Can
Have to**

I		
He		
She		
It	can/can't sing.
We	(cannot)
You		
They		

Can you sing?
Yes, I can.
No, I can't.

Read and practice.

1. Can Mary ski?

2. Can Sam cook Chinese food?

3. Can they play the violin?

4. Can you sing?

5. Can Jeff play chess?

6. Can William play the piano?

7. Can Sally play football?

8. Can they skate?

9. Ask another student in your class: Can you _____?

74

Read and practice.

A. Can Jack fix cars?

B. Of course he can.
He fixes cars every day. He's a mechanic.

1. Can Arthur play the violin?
violinist

2. Can Anita sing?
singer

3. Can Fred and Ginger dance?
dancer

4. Can Stanley cook?
chef

5. Can Lois bake apple pies?
baker

6. Can Richard act?
actor

7. Can Elizabeth and Katherine act?
actress

8. Can Eleanor teach?
teacher

9. Can Shirley drive a truck?
truck driver

10. Can Dan drive a bus?
bus driver

I		
We		
You	} have to	
They		work.
He		
She	} has to	
It		

Herbert is depressed. He's having a party today, but his friends can't go to his party. They're all busy.

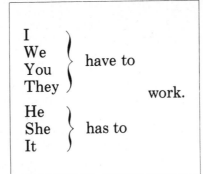

A. Can Michael go to Herbert's party?

B. No, he can't. He has to go to the doctor.

1. *Peggy?*
fix her car

2. *George and Martha?*
go to the supermarket

3. *Nancy?*
go to the dentist

4. *Henry?*
clean his apartment

5. *Carl and Tim?*
do their homework

6. *Linda?*
wash her clothes

7. *Ted?*
go to the bank

8. Can YOU go to Herbert's party?

No, _____.

Read and practice.

Make up conversations with other students in your class.

Include some of these words in your questions.

go to a movie
go to a baseball game
have lunch
have dinner
go swimming
go dancing
go skating
go skiing
go shopping
go bowling
go sailing
go jogging

Include some of these words and others in your answers.

go to the doctor
go to the bank
do my homework
visit a friend in the hospital
work

_____
_____
_____
_____
_____
_____
_____

Future: Going to
Time Expressions
Want to

I am	
He She } is It	going to read.
We You } are They	

am I	
What is { he she it }	going to do?
are { we you they }	

Read and practice.

A. What's Fred going to do today?*

B. He's going to fix his car.

A. What are Mr. and Mrs. Brown going to do tomorrow?†

B. They're going to go to the beach.

*today includes:

this morning
this afternoon
this evening
tonight

† tomorrow includes:

tomorrow morning
tomorrow afternoon
tomorrow evening
tomorrow night

1. What's Mary going to do this morning?

2. What are Carol and Dan going to do tomorrow morning?

3. What are you going to do this afternoon?

4. What's Tom going to do tomorrow afternoon?

5. What are Mr. and Mrs. Smith going to do this evening?

6. What's Jane going to do tomorrow evening?

7. What are you going to do tonight?

8. What's Henry going to do tomorrow night?

9. Ask another student: What are you going to do _____?
   (tomorrow,
   this evening...)

Read and practice.

*Other phrases you can use are:

this/next week, month, year
this/next Sunday, Monday, Tuesday, Wednesday, Thursday, Friday, Saturday
this/next January, February, March, April, May, June, July, August, September,
           October, November, December
this/next spring, summer, fall (autumn), winter

† "Right away," "immediately," and "at once" mean the same as "right now."

1. When are you going to wash your car?

2. When are you going to call your grandmother?

3. When are you going to visit us?

4. When are you going to cut your hair?

5. When are you going to plant flowers this year?

6. When are you going to fix your car?

7. When are you going to write to your Uncle John?

8. Mr. Smith! When are you going to iron those pants?

9. Ask another student: When are you going to _____?

I We You They	} want to	
He She It	} wants to	study.

Read and practice.

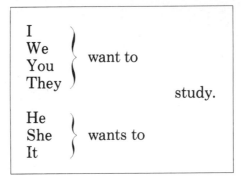

A. What are you going to do tomorrow?

B. I don't know.
I want to **go swimming,** but I think the weather is going to be bad.

A. Really? What's the forecast?

B. The radio says it's going to **rain.**

A. That's strange! According to the newspaper, it's going to **be sunny.**

B. I hope you're right.
I REALLY want to **go swimming.**

1. *have a picnic*
rain
be nice

2. *go skiing*
be warm
snow

3. *go to the beach*
be cloudy
be sunny

4. *plant flowers in my garden*
be very hot
be cool

5. *go sailing*
be foggy
be clear

6. *go to the zoo with my children*
be cold
be warm

Discuss in class.

What's the weather today?
What's the weather forecast for tomorrow?

WHAT TIME IS IT?

It's 11:00.   It's eleven o'clock.

It's 11:15.   It's eleven fifteen.*

It's 11:30.   It's eleven thirty.*

It's 11:45.   It's eleven forty-five.*

It's 12:00.   It's twelve o'clock.

noon   midnight

ON YOUR OWN

Read and practice this conversation.

A. What time does the concert begin?

B. It begins at 8:00.

A. Oh no! I think we're going to be late!

B. Why? What time is it?

A. It's 7:30. And we have to leave RIGHT NOW!

B. I can't leave now. I'm SHAVING!

A. Please try to hurry! I don't want to be late for the concert.

*You can also say:

   11:15 — a quarter after eleven
   11:30 — half past eleven
   11:45 — a quarter to twelve

A. What time does _____?

B. It _____ at _____.

A. Oh no! I think we're going to be late!

B. Why? What time is it?

A. It's _____. And we have to leave RIGHT NOW!

B. I can't leave now. I'm _____!

A. Please try to hurry! I don't want to be late for the _____.

1. What time does the football game begin?
2:00/1:30
taking a bath

2. What time does the plane leave?
4:15/3:45
putting on my clothes

3. What time does the English class begin?
9:00/8:45
getting up

4. What time does the bus leave?
7:00/6:30
packing my suitcase

5. What time does the train leave?
5:15/4:30
taking a shower

6. What time does the play begin?
8:30/8:00
looking for my pants

7. _____

Past Tense: Regular Verbs Introduction to Irregular Verbs

HOW DO YOU FEEL TODAY?

I feel great!

I feel fine.

I feel O.K.

I'm glad to hear that.

So-so.

Not so good.

I feel terrible.

I'm sorry to hear that.

What's the matter with him?
He has a headache.

Ask and answer these questions.

stomachache

toothache

backache

1. _____?

She _____.

2. _____?

He _____.

3. _____?

I _____.

earache

sore throat

cold

4. _____?

He _____.

5. _____?

I _____.

6. _____?

She _____.

Ask another student in your class.

A. How do you feel today?	
B. _____.	
A. I'm glad to hear that.	

A. How do you feel today?

B. _____.

A. What's the matter with you?

B. I have _____.

A. I'm sorry to hear that.

Yesterday I worked.		I work every day.
Yesterday I played the piano.		I play the piano every day.
Yesterday I rested.		I rest every day.

work	– work**ed**	[t]
play	– play**ed**	[d]
rest	– rest**ed**	[id]

WHAT DID YOU DO YESTERDAY?

[t]

1. *I worked*

2. *cook*

3. *talk on the telephone*

4. *fix*

5. *brush*

6. *dance*

7. *smoke*

8. *watch*

[d]

9. *play*

10. *study*

11. *shave*

12. *smile*

13. *clean*

14. *cry*

15. *listen to*

16. *yawn*

[id]

17. *shout*

18. *paint*

19. *wait for*

20. *plant*

Every Day

I We You They	work.
He She It	works.

Yesterday

I We You They He She It	worked.

Read and practice.

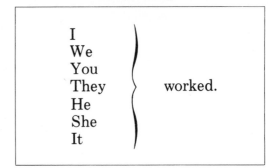

A. How does John feel?
B. Not so good.
A. What's the matter with him?
B. He has a **sore throat.**
A. Why?
B. Because he **smoked** all day.*

*Or: all morning, all afternoon, all evening, all night.

1. *Mary*

2. *George*

3. *you*

4. *Fred*

5. *Mrs. Smith*

6. *you*

7. *David*

8. *you*

9. *Barbara*

Irregular Verbs

eat – ate	sing – sang	drink – drank	sit – sat

10. *Sally*

11. *Mario*

12. *you*

13. *Helen*

14. *you*

15. *Walter*

ON YOUR OWN

You don't feel very well today. Call
your doctor and make an appointment.

A. Hello, Doctor _____. This is _____.

B. Hello, _____. How are you?

A. I don't feel very well today.

B. I'm sorry to hear that. What seems to be the problem?

A. I have a TERRIBLE _____.

B. Do you have any idea why?

A. Well, Doctor . . . I probably have a terrible _____ because I _____ all _____ yesterday.

B. Do you USUALLY _____ all _____?

A. No, I don't. But I _____ all _____ YESTERDAY!

B. Do you want to make an appointment?

A. Yes, I do. When can you see me?

B. How about tomorrow at _____ o'clock?

A. That's fine. Thank you very much.

B. See you tomorrow.

A. Good-bye.

Past Tense:
Yes/No Questions
WH Questions
More Irregular Verbs

I worked.	Did you work?
I didn't work.	Yes, I did.
(did not)	No, I didn't.

Read and practice.

Today includes:

this morning
this afternoon
this evening
tonight

Yesterday includes:

yesterday morning
yesterday afternoon
yesterday evening
last night

1. Did he study English last night?

2. Did she wash her windows this morning?

3. Did you play the piano yesterday afternoon?

4. Did they call the doctor this afternoon?

5. Did she listen to records yesterday morning?

6. Did he clean his bedroom today?

I went.	Did you go?
I didn't go.	Yes, I did.
(did not)	No, I didn't.

Read and practice.

1. Did you go skating yesterday?
go — went

2. Did you take the subway this morning?
take — took

3. Did Steven get up at 10:00 this morning?
get — got

4. Did he have a stomachache last night?
have — had

5. Did Mrs. Smith buy bananas yesterday?
buy — bought

6. Did Tommy write to his grandmother this week?

write — wrote

7. Did you read a book this afternoon?
read — read

8. Did they do their homework last night?
do — did

95

Read and practice.

1. Mary went to a party last night.

2. She got up late today.

3. She missed the bus.

4. She had to walk to the office.

5. She arrived late for work.

6. Her boss shouted at her.

7. She had a terrible headache all afternoon.

Complete this conversation, using the information above.

A. Hi, Mary! Did you have a good day today?

B. No, I didn't. I had a TERRIBLE day.

A. What happened?

B. I had a terrible headache all afternoon.

A. Why did you have a terrible headache all afternoon?

B. Because my boss shouted at me.

A. Why did your boss shout at you?

B. Because I arrived late for work.

A. Why _____ late for work?

B. Because _____.

A. Why _____?

B. Because _____.

A. Why _____?

B. Because _____.

A. Why _____?

B. Because I went to a party last night.

Ask another student in your class.

1. Did you go to a party last night?
2. What did you do last night?
3. Did you get up late today?
4. What time did you get up?
5. How did you get to class today?
6. Did you arrive on time?

More
Irregular Verbs

forget	–	forgot
meet	–	met
steal	–	stole

"EXCUSES! EXCUSES!"

Are you sometimes late for class?
What do you usually tell your teacher?
Here are some excuses you can use next time you're late.

I got up late.

I missed the _____. (bus, train, subway)

I had a _____ this morning. (stomachache, headache . . .)

I had to go to the _____ before class. (post office, bank, doctor, dentist . . .)

I forgot my _____ and had to go back home and get it. (English book, pencil . . .)

I met _____ on the way to class. (an old friend, my cousin . . .)

A thief stole my _____. (car, bicycle . . .)

Add some of your own excuses.

_____

_____

_____

Read and practice.

A. Why are you late for class?
Did you get up late?

B. No, I didn't get up late.

A. Did you have a headache this morning?

B. No, I didn't have a headache this morning.

A. Did you miss the bus?

B. No, I didn't miss the bus.

A. Well, why are you late for class?

B. A thief stole my bicycle.

A. Excuses! Excuses!

Now try this conversation with students in your class, using your own excuses.

A. Why are you late for class?
Did _____?

B. No, _____.

A. Did _____?

B. No, _____.

A. Did _____?

B. No, _____.

A. Well, why are you late for class?

B. _____.

A. Excuses! Excuses!

To Be: Past Tense

<table>
<tr><td>I
He
She
It</td><td>} was</td></tr>
</table>

I / He / She / It } was
happy.
We / You / They } were

Read and practice this commercial for WHAMMO Vitamins.

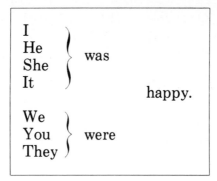

Before our family bought WHAMMO Vitamins, we were always tired.

    I was tired.
    My wife was tired.
    My children were tired, too.

Now we're energetic, because WE bought WHAMMO Vitamins. How about you?

WHAMMO Commercial

Before our family bought _____,

we were always _____.

    I was _____.

    My wife/husband was _____.

    My children were _____, too.

Now we're _____ because WE bought _____.

How about you?

Using the above script, prepare commercials for these other fine WHAMMO products.

1. *sad*   *happy*   2. *hungry*   *full*   3. *dirty*   *clean*

4. *sick*   *healthy*   5. *heavy*   *thin*   6. _____   _____

| I He She It We You They | did/didn't | I He She It | was/wasn't |
| | | We You They | were/weren't |

Read and practice.

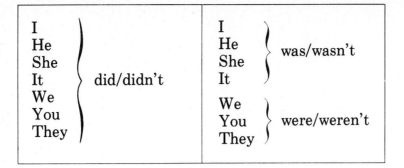

A. Did Tom have a big breakfast today?
B. Yes, he did. He was hungry.

A. Did Jane have a big breakfast today?
B. No, she didn't. She wasn't hungry.

1. Did you sleep well last night?
Yes, _____ tired.

2. Did Roger sleep well last night?
No, _____ tired.

3. Did Mrs. Brown go to the doctor yesterday?
Yes, _____ sick.

4. Did Mr. Brown go to the doctor yesterday?
No, _____ sick.

5. Did Timothy finish his milk?
Yes, _____ thirsty.

6. Did Jennifer finish her milk?
No, _____ thirsty.

7. Did Susan miss the train?
Yes, _____ late.

8. Did Sally miss the train?
No, _____ late.

Yes,	I he she it	was	No,	I he she it	wasn't		
	we you they	were		we you they	weren't		

Yes,	I he she it we you they	did	No,	I he she it we you they	didn't

ON YOUR OWN

Answer these questions and then
ask other students in your class.

DO YOU REMEMBER YOUR CHILDHOOD?

1. What did you look like?
   Were you tall? thin? pretty? handsome? cute?
   Did you have curly hair? straight hair? long hair?
   Did you have dimples? freckles?

2. Did you have many friends?
   What did you do with your friends?
   What games did you play?

3. Did you like school?
   Who was your favorite teacher? Why?
   What was your favorite subject? Why?

4. What did you do in your spare time?
   Did you have a hobby?
   Did you play sports?

5. Who was your favorite hero?

6. How old were you when you began to talk?
   I was _____ years old when I began to talk.
   What were your first words?
   My first words were _____.

7. How old were you when you began to walk?

8. How old were you when you started school?

9. How old were you when you went on your first date?

Add three questions of your own and
ask other students in your class.

10. _____?
11. _____?
12. _____?

Like to
Review of Tenses:
Simple Present
Simple Past
Future: Going to
Indirect Object Pronouns

Read and practice.

A. Are you going to cook spaghetti this week?

B. No, I'm not.
I cooked spaghetti LAST week,* and I don't like to cook spaghetti very often.

*You can also say:

yesterday morning, afternoon, evening
last night

last week, weekend, month, year
last Sunday, Monday, . . . Saturday
last spring, summer, fall (autumn), winter
last January, February, . . . December

1. Are you going to study English this weekend?

2. Are you going to watch TV tonight?

3. Are you going to drink coffee this morning?

4. Is Robert going to buy new clothes this year?

5. Are you going to have dessert this evening?

6. Is Tommy going to play baseball this Saturday?

7. Is Mr. Peterson going to plant flowers this spring?

8. Is Mrs. Johnson going to clean her apartment this week?

9. Are you going to go skiing this February?

10. Is Linda going to travel to Canada this August?

11. Are Mr. and Mrs. Smith going to London this summer?

12. Are you and your friends going to Miami this winter?

> I'm going to give my wife a present.
> I'm going to give her a present.

Read and practice.

A. What are you going to give your wife for her birthday?
Are you going to give her a necklace?

B. No, I can't give her a necklace.
I gave her a necklace LAST YEAR.

A. Are you going to give her flowers?

B. No, I can't give her flowers.
I gave her flowers TWO YEARS AGO.

A. What are you going to do?

B. I don't know. I really have to think about it.

A. What are you going to give your _____ for (his/her) birthday?
Are you going to _____?

B. No, I can't _____. I _____ LAST YEAR.

A. Are you going to _____?

B. No, I can't _____. I _____ TWO YEARS AGO.

A. What are you going to do?

B. I don't know. I really have to think about it.

---

1. *husband*
a new shirt
a necktie

2. *girlfriend*
perfume
a bracelet

3. *boyfriend*
a belt
a sweater

4. *grandmother*
flowers
candy

5. *daughter*
a bicycle
a doll

6.

HARRY! I'M REALLY UPSET!

Read and practice.

Do you know what day this was?
It was my birthday, Harry. And you forgot again.
You didn't send me flowers.
You didn't give me candy.
You didn't buy me a present.
And you didn't even wish me "Happy Birthday."

Happy Birthday, Gladys!

I love you, Harry!

Why Was She Upset With Harry THIS Time?

1. He didn't _____ flowers.
2. _____ candy.
3. _____ a present.
4. _____ "Happy Birthday."

ON YOUR OWN

When is your birthday?
My birthday is _____.*

Tell the class about your last birthday.

What did you do?
Did you receive any presents?
What did you get?
Did your family or friends do anything special for you?
What did they do?

*See page 199 for how to read a date. You can say, for example, January 23rd (twenty-third), November 16th (sixteenth), June 9th (ninth).

Count/Non-Count Nouns

WHAT'S IN HENRY'S KITCHEN?

Count Nouns	Non-Count Nouns
tomatoes	cheese
eggs	milk
bananas	ice cream
apples	bread

Add foods from YOUR kitchen.

Let's make sandwiches for lunch!

Sorry, we can't. There **isn't** any **bread**.

Let's make an apple pie for dessert!

Sorry, we can't. There **aren't** any **apples**.

1. Let's make a salad for dinner!

Sorry _____ lettuce.

2. Let's make an omelette for breakfast!

Sorry _____ eggs.

3. Let's make some fresh lemonade!

Sorry _____ lemons.

4. Let's bake a cake for dessert!

Sorry _____ flour.

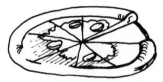

5. Let's make pizza for lunch!

Sorry _____ cheese.

6. Let's make some fresh orange juice for breakfast!

Sorry _____ oranges.

7. Let's make chicken and rice for dinner!

Sorry _____ chicken.

8. Let's have french fries with our hamburgers!

Sorry _____ potatoes.

9. Let's _____!

Sorry _____.

much	many
how much?	how many?
too much	too many
so much that	so many that

A. You look terrible! What's the matter?

B. I drank TOO MUCH milk this morning.

A. HOW MUCH milk did you drink?

B. I drank SO MUCH milk that I'm never going to drink milk again!

A. You look terrible! What's the matter?

B. I ate TOO MANY cookies last night.

A. HOW MANY cookies did you eat?

B. I ate SO MANY cookies that I'm never going to eat a cookie again!

1. *drink . . . coffee*

2. *eat . . . tomatoes*

3. *buy . . . lettuce*

4. *smoke . . . cigarettes*

5. *wash . . . dishes*

6. *drink . . . wine*

7. *write . . . letters*

8. *have . . . ice cream*

9. *sing . . . songs*

10. *read . . . books*

11. *eat . . . cheese*

12. _____

a little	a few
coffee ice cream butter	apples eggs oranges

A. How do you like the _____?

B. I think (it's/they're) delicious.

A. I'm glad you like (it/them). Would you care for some more?

B. Yes, please. But not (too much/too many). Just (a little/a few).
My doctor says that (too much/too many) _____ (is/are) bad for my health.

Try this conversation with other students in your class, using these foods and others.

1. *potatoes*

2. *chocolate cake*

3. *ice cream*

4. *cookies*

5. [   ]

20

Partitives
Count/Non-Count Nouns
Imperatives

My Shopping List

- a can of beans
- a jar of jam
- a bottle of soda
- a box of cereal
- a bag of flour
- a loaf of white bread
- 2 loaves of whole wheat bread
- a bunch of bananas
- 2 bunches of carrots
- a head of lettuce
- a lb.* of butter
- ½ lb.* of cheese

- a quart of milk
- a pack of cigarettes
- a dozen eggs

*a lb. = a pound; ½ lb. = a half pound, or half a pound.

What did YOU buy the last time you went shopping?

A. I'm going to the supermarket. Can I get anything for you?

B. Yes, I need some **bread.**

A. How many **loaves of bread** do you need?

B. Just one **loaf,** please.

1. *cereal*

2. *marmalade*

3. *soda*

4. *bananas*

5. *vegetable soup*

6. *whole wheat bread*

7. *flour*

8.

A. How much does **a head of lettuce** cost?

B. **A head of lettuce** costs **ninety-five cents** (95¢).*

A. **NINETY-FIVE CENTS?!** That's a lot of money!

B. You're right.
Lettuce is very expensive this week.

*25¢ = twenty-five cents
50¢ = fifty cents

    etc.

A. How much does **a pound of apples** cost?

B. **A pound of apples** costs **a dollar twenty-five** ($1.25).†

A. **A DOLLAR TWENTY-FIVE?!** That's a lot of money!

B. You're right.
Apples are very expensive this week.

†$1.00 = a dollar
 $1.50 = a dollar fifty
 $2.25 = two twenty-five
 $4.50 = four fifty

    etc.

1. *butter*

2. *carrots*

3. *milk*

4. *onions*

5. *Swiss cheese*

6. *bananas*

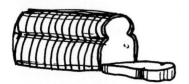

7. *white bread*

8. *oranges*

9.

AT THE RESTAURANT

A. What would you like **for dessert?**

B. I can't decide. What do you recommend?

A. I recommend our **chocolate ice cream.** Everybody says **it's** delicious.*

B. O.K. Please give me **a dish of chocolate ice cream.**

A. What would you like **for breakfast**?

B. I can't decide. What do you recommend?

A. I recommend our **scrambled eggs.** Everybody says **they're** out of this world.*

B. O.K. Please give me **an order of scrambled eggs.**

*Instead of delicious, you can also say:

fantastic
wonderful
magnificent
excellent
out of this world

What would you like . . .

1. . . . for dessert?
(a piece of) apple pie

2. . . . for lunch?
(a bowl of) chicken soup

3. . . . to drink?
(a cup of) coffee

4. . . . for breakfast?
(an order of) pancakes

5. . . . to drink?
(a glass of) red wine

6. . . . for dessert?
(a dish of) vanilla ice cream

7. . . . to drink?
(a cup of) hot chocolate

8. . . . for dessert?
(a bowl of) strawberries

9.

STANLEY'S FAVORITE RECIPES

Are you going to have a party soon? Do you want to cook something special? Stanley the chef recommends this recipe for VEGETABLE STEW. This is Stanley's favorite recipe for vegetable stew, and everybody says it's fantastic!

1. Put **a little butter** into a saucepan.

2. Chop up **a few onions.**

3. Cut up **(a little/a few)** _____

4. Pour in _____

5. Slice _____

6. Add _____

7. Chop up ___

8. Slice _____

9. Add _____

10. Cook for 3 hours.

When is your English teacher's birthday? Do you want to bake a special cake? Stanley the chef recommends this recipe for FRUITCAKE. This is Stanley's favorite recipe for fruitcake, and everybody says it's out of this world!

1. Put 3 cups of flour into a mixing bowl.

2. Add **a little sugar.**

3. Slice **(a little/a few)** _____

4. Cut up _____

5. Pour in _____

6. Add _____

7. Chop up ___

8. Add _____

9. Mix in _____

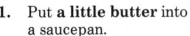

10. Bake for 45 minutes.

ON YOUR OWN

Do you have a favorite recipe?
Share it with other students in your class.

Future Tense: Will
Prepositions of Time
Might

I	will	I'll	
He	will	He'll	
She	will	She'll	
It	will →	It'll	work.
We	will	We'll	
You	will	You'll	
They	will	They'll	

Will he work?
Yes, he will.

A. Will the train arrive soon?

B. Yes, it will. It'll arrive in five minutes.

1. Will the soup be ready soon?
_____ in a few minutes.

2. Will Miss Blake be back soon?
_____ in an hour.

3. Will David finish school soon?
_____ in a month.

4. Will the tomatoes be ripe soon?
_____ in a few weeks.

5. Will Dr. Smith be here soon?
_____ in half an hour.

6. Will you get married soon?
_____ in a few months.

7. Will you be ready soon?
_____ in a few seconds.

8. Will the concert begin soon?
_____ at seven o'clock.

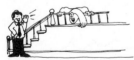

9. Will Mrs. Green be home soon?
_____ in a little while.

10. Will the flowers bloom soon?
_____ in April.

11. Will Betty get out of the hospital soon?
_____ in a few days.

12. Will Frank get out of jail soon?
_____ in a few months.

I He She It We You They } will work.	I He She It We You They } won't work. (will not)

WHAT DO YOU THINK?

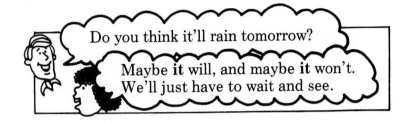

Do you think it'll rain tomorrow?

Maybe **it** will, and maybe **it** won't. We'll just have to wait and see.

1. Do you think Cynthia will marry Norman?

2. Do you think it'll be very cold this winter?

3. Do you think you'll be happy in your new neighborhood?

4. Do you think Mary's husband will find a new job?

5. Do you think I'll be famous some day?

6. Do you think they'll have a baby soon?

7. Do you think there will be many people at the beach tomorrow?

8. Do you think we'll have to fight in a war some day?

9. Do you think _____?

I	
He	
She	
It	might move to New York.
We	
You	
They	

A. When are you going to move to New York?

B. I don't know.
I might move to New York in a few weeks,
or I might move to New York in a few months.
I really can't decide.

A. Where are you going to go for your vacation?

B. We don't know.
We might go to Mexico, or we might go to Japan.
We really can't decide.

1. What kind of food is he going to cook tonight?

3. When are you going to clean your apartment?

5. What are they going to do tonight?

7. What are you going to buy your brother for his birthday?

9. How are you going to come to class tomorrow?

2. What color is she going to paint her kitchen?

4. What are they going to name their new daughter?

6. When are you two going to get married?

8. What is he going to name his new puppy?

10. What are you going to be when you grow up?

THE OPTIMIST AND THE PESSIMIST

A. Would you like to **go swimming** with me?

B. No, I don't think so.

A. Why not?

B. I'm afraid I might **drown.**

A. Don't worry! You won't **drown.**

B. Are you sure?

A. Yes, I'm positive!

B. O.K. I'll **go swimming** with you.

1. *go skiing*
break my leg

2. *go to a fancy restaurant*
get sick

3. *sit in the sun*
get a sunburn

4. *go dancing*
step on your feet

5. *take a walk in the park*
catch a cold

6. *go to Jack's party*
have a terrible time

7. *go sailing*
get seasick

8. *take a ride in the country*
get carsick

9. *share a bottle of wine*
get drunk

10. *go to the movies*
fall asleep

11. *go to a lecture*
be bored

12.

ON YOUR OWN

Be a pessimist! Using <u>might</u>, <u>might not</u>,
<u>will</u>, <u>won't</u>, answer these questions.

1. Why don't you want to go to a party tonight?
2. Why don't you want to have dinner at a fancy restaurant?
3. Why don't you want to go to the movies tonight?
4. Why don't you want to buy a new car?

Comparatives
Should
Possessive Pronouns

cold – colder	large – larger	big – bigger	easy – easier
short – shorter	safe – safer	hot – hotter	busy – busier

A. I think you'll like my new apartment.

B. But I liked your OLD apartment. It was **large.**

A. That's right. But my new apartment is **larger.**

1. *bicycle*
fast

2. *refrigerator*
big

3. *car*
shiny

4. *dog*
friendly

5. *neighborhood*
safe

6. *living room rug*
soft

7. *sports car*
fancy

8. *recipe for vegetable stew*
easy

9. *wig*
pretty

cold – colder	interesting – more interesting
large – larger	intelligent – more intelligent
big – bigger	comfortable – more comfortable
easy – easier	beautiful – more beautiful

A. I think you'll like my new rocking chair.

B. But I liked your OLD rocking chair. It was **comfortable**.

A. That's right. But my new rocking chair is **more comfortable**.

1. *girlfriend*
intelligent

2. *boyfriend*
handsome

3. *watch*
accurate

4. *kitchen sink*
large

5. *house*
beautiful

6. *sofa*
attractive

7. *English teacher*
smart

8. *roommate*
interesting

9. *boss*
nice

10. *tennis racket*
light

11. *recipe for fruitcake*
delicious

12.

<table>
<tr><td>I
He
She
It
We
You
They</td><td>should study.</td></tr>
</table>

Should I study?

A. Should I buy a bicycle or a motorcycle?

B. I think you should buy a bicycle.

A. Why?*

B. Bicycles are **safer than** motorcycles.

A. Should he study English or Latin?

B. I think he should study English.

A. Why?*

B. English is **more useful than** Latin.

*Or: Why do you say that? What makes you say that? How come?

1. Should I buy a dog or a cat?

2. Should he buy a used car or a new car?

3. Should I vote for John Black or Peter Smith?

4. Should he go out on a date with Doris or Jane?

5. Should she go out on a date with Roger or Bill?

6. Should they buy a black-and-white TV or a color TV?

7. Should we buy this fan or that fan?

8. Should she buy these earrings or those earrings?

9. Should I plant flowers or vegetables this spring?

10. Should he study the piano with Mrs. Wong or Miss Schultz?

11. Should I buy the hat in my left hand or the hat in my right hand?

12. Should they go to the cafeteria up the street or the cafeteria down the street?

13. Should she buy fur gloves or leather gloves?

14. Should I go to the laundromat across the street or the laundromat around the corner?

15. Should I hire Miss Jones or Miss Wilson?

16. Should I fire Mr. Jackson or Mr. Brown?

17.

my	– mine	our	– ours
his	– his	your	– yours
her	– hers	their	– theirs

A. I'm jealous!
My dog isn't as friendly as your dog.

B. Don't be ridiculous!
Yours is MUCH friendlier than **mine.**

A. I'm jealous!
My novels aren't as interesting as Ernest Hemingway's novels.

B. Don't be ridiculous!
Yours are MUCH more interesting than **his.**

fast

1. *my car*
your car

comfortable

2. *my furniture*
your furniture

long

3. *my hair*
Rita's hair

nice

4. *my boss*
your boss

intelligent

5. *my children*
your children

big

6. *my house*
the Jones's house

clean

7. *my apartment*
your apartment

good-better

8. *my pronunciation*
Maria's pronunciation

delicious

9. *my recipe for fruitcake*
Stanley's recipe for fruitcake

popular

10. *my songs*
the Beatles' songs

important

11. *my job*
the President's job

12.

Read and practice.

In my opinion, New York is more interesting than San Francisco.

I disagree. I think San Francisco is MUCH more interesting than New York.

Do you think the weather in Miami is better than the weather in Honolulu?

No, I don't think so. I think the weather in Honolulu is MUCH better than the weather in Miami.

Are the people in Centerville as friendly as the people in Greenville?

No, the people in Centerville aren't as friendly as the people in Greenville, but they're more interesting. Do you agree?

Yes, I agree.

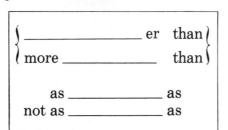

$$\left\{ \begin{array}{l} \underline{\hspace{2cm}} \text{ er } \quad \text{than} \\ \text{more} \underline{\hspace{2cm}} \quad \text{than} \end{array} \right\}$$

as \underline{\hspace{2cm}} as
not as \underline{\hspace{2cm}} as

Talk with other students about two cities: your home town and the city you live in now, or any two cities you know. Talk about . . .

the streets: quiet, safe, clean, wide, busy . . . ?
the buildings: high, modern, pretty . . . ?
the weather: cold, warm, rainy, snowy . . . ?
the people: friendly, nice, polite, honest, busy, happy, hospitable,
           talkative, healthy, wealthy, poor . . . ?
the city in general: large, interesting, lively, exciting, expensive . . . ?

In your conversation you might want to use some of these expressions:

I agree.
I disagree.
I agree/disagree with (you, him, her, John . . .).

I think so.
I don't think so.
In my opinion, . . .

23

Superlatives

kind – the kindest cold – the coldest	nice – the nicest safe – the safest
busy – the busiest happy – the happiest	big – the biggest hot – the hottest

A. I think your friend Margaret is very **nice.**

B. She certainly is. She's **the nicest** person I know.

1. I think your cousin is very **friendly.**

2. I think your Uncle George is very **funny.**

3. I think your parents are very **kind.**

4. I think your older brother is very **shy.**

5. I think your cousin Nancy is very **pretty.**

6. I think Larry is very **lazy.**

7. I think the students in our class are very **smart.**

8. I think your Aunt Gertrude is very **cold.**

9. I think your younger brother is very **sloppy.**

kind – the kindest busy – the busiest nice – the nicest big – the biggest	talented – the most talented energetic – the most energetic interesting – the most interesting polite – the most polite

A. I think your grandmother is very **energetic.**

B. She certainly is.
She's **the most energetic** person I know.

1. I think your son is very **polite.**

2. I think John is very **stubborn.**

I think our English teacher is very **patient.**

3.

4. I think your younger sister is very **talented.**

5. I think your older sister is very **bright.**

6. I think your upstairs neighbor is very **noisy.**

7. I think your downstairs neighbor is very **boring.**

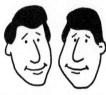

8. I think your twin brothers are very **nice.**

9. I think your grandfather is very **generous.**

10. I think Walter is very **stingy.**

11. I think your girlfriend is very **honest.**

12.

a cheap typewriter	a comfortable chair	a good car
a cheaper typewriter	a more comfortable chair	a better car
the cheapest typewriter	the most comfortable chair	the best car

Read and practice.

IN THE DEPARTMENT STORE

A. May I help you?

B. Yes, please. I want to buy a **cheap** typewriter.

A. I think you'll like this one. It's VERY **cheap.**

B. Don't you have a **cheaper** typewriter?

A. No, I'm afraid not.
This is **the cheapest** one we have.

B. Thank you anyway.

A. Sorry we can't help you. Please come again.

A. May I help you?

B. Yes, please. I want to buy a/an _____ _____.

A. I think you'll like this one. It's VERY _____.

B. Don't you have a/an { _____er } _____?
  { more _____ }

A. No, I'm afraid not.
  This is the { _____est } one we have.
  { most_____ }

B. Thank you anyway.

A. Sorry we can't help you. Please come again.

1. *large refrigerator*

2. *comfortable rocking chair*

3. *good record player*

4. *fancy necktie*

5. *cheap watch*

6. *small kitchen table*

7. *good tape recorder*

8. *light tennis racket*

9. *elegant evening gown*

10. *modern sofa*

11. *short novel*

12.

good	bad
better	worse
best	worst

Answer these questions and then ask another student in your class. Give reasons for your opinions.

In your opinion . . .

1. Who is the most popular actor/actress in your country?

2. Who is the most popular TV star?

3. Who is the best singer? (What kind of songs does he/she sing?)

4. Who are the wealthiest people in your country? (What do they do for a living? Where do they live?)

5. Who is the most important person in your country now? (What does he/she do?)

6. Who is the most important person in the history of your country? (What did he/she do?)

In your opinion . . .

7. What is the best city in your country? Why?

8. What is the worst city in your country? Why?

9. What are the most interesting tourist sights for visitors to your country? (museums, monuments, churches . . .)

10. What are the most popular vacation places for people in your country? Why?

In your opinion . . .

11. What is the most popular car in your country?

12. What is the most popular sport?

13. What is the funniest TV program?

14. What is the best newspaper?

15. What is the most popular magazine?

16. What is the most popular food? (Do you know how to make it? If you know an easy recipe, share it with the students in your class.)

24

Directions

MAIN ST.

drug store	laundromat
barber shop	butcher shop
bakery	shoe store
library	clinic
police station	high school
bank	post office

laundromat?

A. Excuse me. Would you please tell me how to get to the laundromat from here?

B. **Walk up** Main Street and you'll see the laundromat **on the right, across from** the drugstore.

post office?

A. Excuse me. Would you please tell me how to get to the post office from here?

B. **Walk down** Main Street and you'll see the post office **on the left, next to** the high school.

1. *shoe store?*

2. *police station?*

3. *high school?*

4. *barber shop?*

5. *butcher shop?*

6. *bank?*

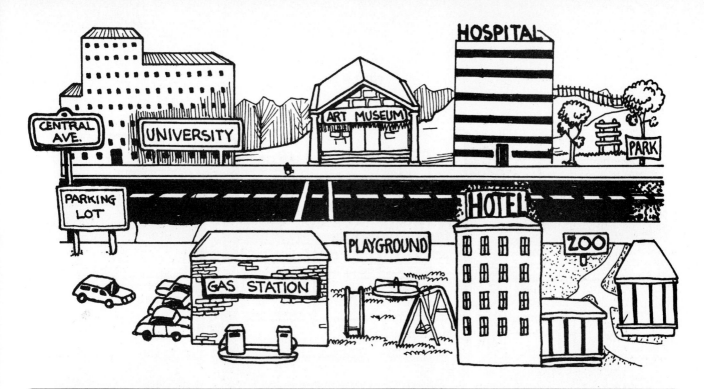

A. Excuse me. Would you please tell me how to get to the hospital from here?

B. **Walk along** Central Avenue and you'll see the hospital **on the left, between** the art museum and the park.

hospital?

1. *parking lot?*

2. *university?*

3. *park?*

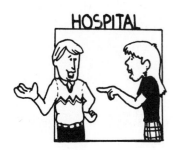

4. *art museum?*

5. *playground?*

6. *zoo?*

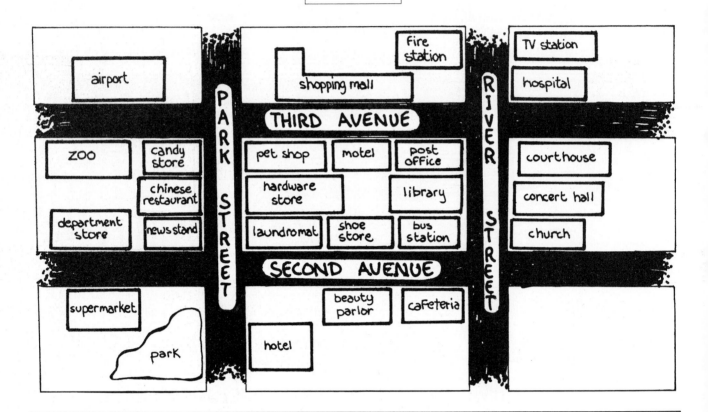

bus station?

A. Excuse me. Would you please tell me how to get to the bus station from here?

B. **Walk up** Park Street to Second Avenue and **turn right. Walk along** Second Avenue and you'll see the bus station **on the left, across from** the cafeteria.

concert hall?

A. Excuse me. Would you please tell me how to get to the concert hall from here?

B. **Drive along** Second Avenue to River Street and **turn left. Drive up** River Street and you'll see the concert hall **on the right, between** the courthouse and the church.

1. *shopping mall?*

2. *hardware store?*

3. *library?*

4. *zoo?*

5. *department store?*

6. *TV station?*

7. *hospital?*

8.

Take the bus and get off at Main Street.

A. Excuse me. What's the quickest way to get to Peter's Pet Shop?

B. **Take** the Main Street Bus and **get off** at First Avenue.
Walk up First Avenue and you'll see Peter's Pet Shop **on the right.**

A. Thank you for your help.

B. You're welcome.

A. Excuse me. What's the easiest way to get to Harry's Barber Shop?

B. **Take** the subway and **get off** at Fourth Avenue.
Walk down Fourth Avenue and you'll see Harry's Barber Shop **on the left.**

A. Thank you for your help.

B. You're welcome.

1. What's the fastest way to get to the baseball stadium?

2. What's the best way to get to St. Andrew's Church?

3. What's the most direct way to get to the zoo?

4. I'm in a hurry! What's the shortest way to get to the train station?

Read and practice.

GETTING AROUND TOWN

A. Can you recommend **a good hotel**?

B. Yes. The Bellview is **a good hotel**.
I think it's **one of the best hotels** in town.

A. Can you tell me how to get there?

B. Sure. Take the subway and get off at Brighton Boulevard. You'll see The Bellview at the corner of Brighton Boulevard and Twelfth Street.

A. Thank you very much.

B. You're welcome.

These people are visiting your city. Using the above conversation as a guide, help these people "get around town." Recommend real places you know and like, and give directions. If you disagree with another student's recommendation, explain why and recommend another place.

1. *a good restaurant?*   **2.** *a cheap department store?*   **3.** *a quiet, romantic cafe?*

4.

Adverbs
Comparative of Adverbs
Agent Nouns
If-Clauses

slow – slowly bad – badly beautiful – beautifully	terrible – terribly miserable – miserably simple – simply	sloppy – sloppily busy – busily lazy – lazily	fast – fast hard – hard good – well

> work – a worker
play – a player
drive – a driver

A. I think he's **a careless driver.**

B. I agree. He **drives VERY carelessly**.

1. *a careless skier*

2. *a slow chess player*

3. *a beautiful singer*

4. *sloppy painters*

5. *an accurate translator*

6. *a good teacher*

7. *careful workers*

8. *a graceful dancer*

9. *good tennis players*

10. *dishonest card players*

11. *a fast driver*

12. *a hard worker*

softly – { softer / more softly }

loud(ly) – { louder / more loudly }

slowly – { slower / more slowly }

neatly – { neater / more neatly }

carefully – more carefully
politely – more politely

hard – harder
fast – faster
early – earlier
late – later

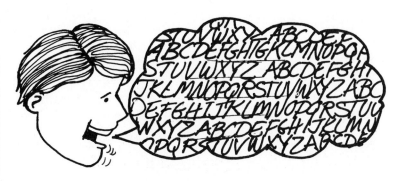

A. Bob speaks VERY **quickly**.

B. You're right. He should try to speak { **slower** / **more slowly** }.

1. Linda speaks very softly.

2. Ronald goes to bed very late.

3. Janet skates very carelessly.

4. Your friends come to class very early.

5. David types very slowly.

6. They dress very sloppily.

7. Peter speaks to his parents very impolitely.

8. Karen plays her record player very loud(ly).

9. They work very slowly.

If _____ will _____

What are they going to name their new baby?

If they have a boy, they'll name him John.
If they have a girl, they'll name her Jane.

1. How are you going to get to school tomorrow?

If it rains, I'll _____.

If it's sunny, I'll _____.

2. What's Bob going to do this Saturday afternoon?

If the weather is good, he'll _____.

If the weather is bad, he'll _____.

3. What's Carmen going to have for dinner tonight?

If she's very hungry, _____.

If she isn't very hungry, _____.

4. What's Fred going to do tomorrow?

If he feels better, _____.

If he doesn't feel better, _____.

5. When are you going to go to sleep tonight?

If I'm tired, _____.

If I'm not tired, _____.

6. What are they going to wear tomorrow?

If it's hot, _____.

If it's cool, _____.

Answer these questions and ask another student in your class.

1. What are you going to do tonight if you have a lot of homework?

2. What are you going to do tonight if you DON'T have a lot of homework?

3. What are you going to have for breakfast tomorrow if you're very hungry?

4. What are you going to have for breakfast tomorrow if you AREN'T very hungry?

5. What are you going to do this weekend if the weather is nice?

6. What are you going to do this weekend if the weather is bad?

EVERYBODY GIVES ME ADVICE

   A.   Everybody tells me I shouldn't drive **so fast**.

   B.   They're right.
       If you drive **too fast**, you might **have an accident**.

1. My boss tells me I shouldn't work so slowly.
lose your job

2. My music teacher says I shouldn't sing so loud.
get a sore throat

3. My friends tell me I shouldn't worry so much.
get an ulcer

4. My dentist says I shouldn't eat so much candy.
get a toothache

5. My teacher told me I shouldn't do my homework so carelessly.
make too many mistakes

6. Our baby-sitter says we shouldn't go to bed so late.
be tired in the morning

7. My parents tell me I shouldn't watch so many scary TV programs.
have nightmares

8. Everybody tells me I shouldn't

_____.

They're right. If _____.

Read and practice.

SUPERSTITIONS

Many people believe that you'll have GOOD luck

if you find a four-leaf clover.
if you find a horseshoe.
if you give a new pair of shoes to a poor person.

You'll have BAD luck

if a black cat walks in front of you.
if you walk under a ladder.
if you open an umbrella in your house.
if you put your shoes on a table.
if you light three cigarettes with one match.

Here are some other superstitions.

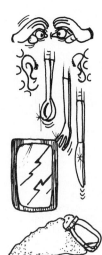

If your right eye itches, you'll laugh soon.
If your left eye itches, you'll cry soon.

If your right ear itches, somebody is saying good things about you.
If your left ear itches, somebody is saying bad things about you.

If a knife falls, a man will visit soon.
If a fork falls, a woman will visit soon.
If a spoon falls, a baby or a fool will visit soon.

If you break a mirror, you'll have bad luck for seven years.

If you spill salt, you should throw a little salt over your left shoulder.
If you don't, you'll have bad luck.

Do you know any superstitions?
Share them with other students in your class.

Act this out in class.

PLEASE DON'T ASK ME A DIFFICULT QUESTION!

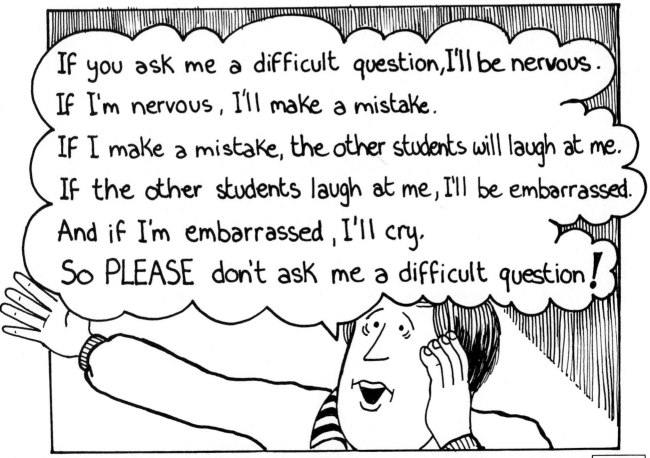

Past Continuous Tense
Reflexive Pronouns
While-Clauses

I			
He			
She	}	was	
It			working.
We			
You	}	were	
They			

THE BLACKOUT

Last night at 8:00 there was a blackout in Centerville. The lights went out all over town.

A. What was Doris doing last night when the lights went out?

B. She was taking a bath.

A. What were Mr. and Mrs. Green doing last night when the lights went out?

B. They were riding in an elevator.

Ask about these people.

1. *Ted*

2. *Irene*

3. *Bob and Judy*

4. *you*

5. *Joe*

6. *your parents*

7. *your younger sister*

8. *your father*

9. *Mr. and Mrs. Jones*

What were YOU doing last night at 8:00? Tell the other students in your class.

A. I saw you yesterday, but you didn't see me.

B. Really? When?

A. At about 2:30.
You were **getting out of a taxi on Main Street**.

B. That wasn't me.
Yesterday at 2:30 I was **cooking dinner**.

A. I guess I made a mistake.

1. *walking into the post office*
fixing my car

2. *walking out of the laundromat*
cleaning my apartment

3. *getting on a bus*
watching TV

4. *getting off a merry-go-round*
playing baseball

5. *jogging through the park*
playing tennis

6. *riding your bicycle along Main St.*
cooking

7. *getting out of a police car*
sleeping

8.

I	myself
you	yourself
he	himself
she	herself
it	itself
we	ourselves
you	yourselves
they	themselves

A. What did **John** do yesterday?

B. He went to the movies.

A. Who did he go to the movies with?

B. Nobody. He went to the movies **by himself**.

1. *Patty*
go to the beach

2. *Peter*
go to the ballgame

3. *you*
go bowling

4. *you and your wife*
play cards

5. *Mr. and Mrs. Jones*
have a picnic

6. *Mrs. Wilson*
drive to New York

7. *you*
go to Bob's party

8. *Mr. Wilson*
take a walk in the park

9.

A. You look upset.

B. Yes. I had a bad day today.

A. Why? What happened?

B. I **lost my wallet** while I was **jogging through the park.**

A. I'm sorry to hear that.*

A. Harry looks upset.

B. Yes. He had a bad day today.

A. Why? What happened?

B. He **cut himself** while he was **shaving**.

A. That's too bad.*

*Or: How awful! That's terrible! What a shame! What a pity!

1. *you*
burned myself
cooking dinner

2. *Sheila*
dropped her packages
walking out of the supermarket

3. *Tom*
hurt himself
playing basketball

4. *your parents*
got a flat tire
driving over a bridge

5. *you*
fainted
waiting for the bus

6. *Nelson*
saw a few gray hairs
looking at himself in the mirror

7. *you and your wife*
had an accident
driving home

8. *Linda*
cut herself
slicing a tomato

9. *you*
a dog bit me
standing on the corner

10. *Marvin*
tripped and fell
walking to work

11. *your aunt and uncle*
somebody stole their car
shopping

12. *you*
a can of paint fell on me
walking under a ladder

ON YOUR OWN

Everybody has a bad day once in a while. Try to remember a few days when something bad happened to you. What happened? And what were you doing when it happened? Share your sad stories with the other students in your class.

27

Could
Be Able to
Have Got to
Too + Adjective

I He She It We You They	can/can't	could/couldn't study.

Could he study?
Yes, he could.
No, he couldn't.

A. Could Peter play on the basketball team when he was a little boy?

B. No, he couldn't.
He was **too short**.

1. Could Henry go to work yesterday?
sick

2. Could Rita go out with her boyfriend last weekend?
busy

3. Could Mr. and Mrs. Jones finish their dinner?
full

4. Could Billy buy a drink at the bar last Saturday night?
young

5. Could you finish your homework last night?
tired

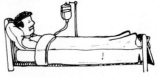

6. Could Frank get out of bed the day after his operation?
weak

7. Could Betty tell the policeman about her accident?
upset

8. Could Stuart eat at his wedding?
nervous

$$\text{could} = \left\{\begin{array}{l}\text{was}\\\text{were}\end{array}\right\} \text{able to}$$

$$\text{couldn't} = \left\{\begin{array}{l}\text{wasn't}\\\text{weren't}\end{array}\right\} \text{able to}$$

ARRIVALS

A. Was Jimmy able to lift his grandmother's suitcase?

B. No, he wasn't able to. It was **too heavy.**

1. Was Louise able to paint her house yesterday afternoon?
windy

2. Was Carl able to sit down on the bus this morning?
crowded

3. Were Mr. and Mrs. Johnson able to go swimming in the ocean during their vacation?
cold

4. Was Shirley able to finish her order of spaghetti and meatballs?
spicy

5. Was Tom able to find his wallet last night?
dark

6. Were you able to do the grammar exercises last night?
difficult

7. Could Jeff and Gloria see the full moon last night?
cloudy

8. Was Willy able to wear his brother's suit to the dance last Saturday night?
small

A. Did Barbara enjoy herself at the concert last night?

B. Unfortunately, she { wasn't able to / couldn't } go to the concert last night. She had to **study for an examination**.

1. Did Ronald enjoy himself at the baseball game yesterday?
go to the dentist

2. Did you enjoy yourself at the tennis match last week?
visit my boss in the hospital

3. Did Mr. and Mrs. Wilson enjoy themselves at the symphony yesterday evening?
wait for the plumber

4. Did Sally enjoy herself at the theater last Saturday night?
take care of her little brother

5. Did you enjoy yourself at the discotheque last night?
finish my homework

6. Did Fred enjoy himself at Mary's party last Friday evening?
work late at the office

7. Did you and your classmates enjoy yourselves at the movies last night?
study English

8. Did Marion enjoy herself at the picnic last Sunday?
take care of her neighbor's dog

9. Did you enjoy yourself at the football game yesterday?
fix a flat tire

10.

| I've (I have) We've (we have) You've (you have) They've (they have) | got to = | I We You They | have to |
| He's (he has) She's (she has) It's (it has) | got to = | He She It | has to |

work.

Read and practice.

A. I'm afraid I won't be able to help you **move to your new apartment** tomorrow.

B. You won't? Why not?

A. I've got to **take my son to the doctor.**

B. Don't worry about it!
I'm sure I'll be able to **move to my new apartment** by myself.

A. I'm afraid I won't be able to help you _____ tomorrow.

B. You won't? Why not?

A. I've got to _____.

B. Don't worry about it!
I'm sure I'll be able to _____ by myself.

1. *clean your garage*
go to the bank

2. *paint your living room*
fly to Chicago

3. *fix your car*
drive my husband to the clinic

4. *do your homework*
practice the piano

5. *repair your kitchen window*
take care of my neighbor's baby

6. *cook Christmas dinner*
buy presents for my children

7. *study for the examination*
take my daughter to her ballet lesson

8. *take Jennifer to the dentist*
work late at the office

9. *take Rover to the vet*
visit my mother in the hospital

10.

Read and practice.

1.
George is upset.
He got a flat tire and he won't be able
to get to the airport on time.

2.
Rita is frustrated.
She lost her key and she can't get into
her apartment.

3.
Mrs. Brown's English class is really
upset.
Mrs. Brown is sick and she won't be able
to teach them English this week.

4.
Sidney is disappointed.
He wasn't able to find a job in New York
City and he had to move home with his
mother and father.

5.
Ted was really disappointed last year.
He couldn't dance in the school play.
His teacher said he was too clumsy.

**Are you frustrated, disappointed, or
upset about something? Tell the
class about your problem. If you
don't have a problem now, tell the
class about the LAST time you were
frustrated, disappointed, or upset.**

Must
Must vs. Should
Fewer/Less
Past Tense Review

I		
He		
She		
It	}	must work.
We		
You		
They		

more/less	more/fewer
bread	cookies
fish	potatoes
fruit	eggs

Henry's Diet	
⊖	⊕
bread	fish
cookies	vegetables
candy	fruit
potato chips	
other snack foods	

1. Henry had his yearly checkup today. The doctor told him he's a little too heavy and gave him this diet:

He must eat **less** bread, **fewer** cookies, **less** candy, and **fewer** potato chips and other snack foods.

Also, he must eat **more** fish, **more** vegetables, and **more** fruit.

Shirley's Diet	
⊖	⊕
fatty meat	lean meat
potatoes	grapefruit
rice	green vegetables
rich desserts	

2. Shirley also had her annual checkup today. Her doctor gave her this diet:

She must eat _____

_____

_____

Arthur's Diet	
⊖	⊕
butter	margarine
eggs	skim milk
cheese	yogurt
ice cream	

3. Arthur was worried about his heart. He went to his doctor for an examination and the doctor told him to eat fewer fatty foods.

He must eat/drink _____

_____

_____

Rover's Diet	
⊖	⊕
fatty meat	lean meat
dog biscuits	water

4. Rover went to the vet yesterday for his yearly checkup. The vet told him he's a little too heavy and gave him this diet:

He must eat/drink _____

_____

_____

MY DIET	
⊖	⊕

5. You went to the doctor today for your annual physical examination. The doctor told you you're a little overweight and said you must go on a diet.

I must eat/drink _____

_____

_____

A. I had my yearly checkup today.

B. What did the doctor say?

A. He/She told me I'm a little too heavy and I must lose some weight.

B. Do you have to stop eating _____?

A. No, I don't have to stop eating _____, but I mustn't eat as (much/many) _____ as I did before.

1.

2.

3.

4.

5.

6.

7.

8.

9.

THE CHECKUP

Read and practice.

Hello, Roger. Maybe you can help me.
I want to get a medical checkup, but my doctor moved away.

You should go to MY doctor . . . Dr. Anderson.
He'll give you a very complete examination.

1.  The nurse will lead you into one of the examination rooms.

2. You'll take off your clothes and put on a hospital gown.

3.  Dr. Anderson will come in, shake your hand, and say "hello."

4.  You'll stand on his scale so he can measure your height and your weight.

5.  He'll take your pulse.

6.  Then he'll take your blood pressure.

7. After he takes your blood pressure, he'll take some blood for a blood analysis.

8.  He'll examine your eyes, ears, nose, and throat.

9.  He'll listen to your heart with a stethoscope.

10.  Then he'll take a chest X-ray and do a cardiogram (EKG).

YOUR CHECKUP

You had a complete physical
examination yesterday. Tell us about
your visit to the doctor.

1. The nurse **led** me _____.

2. _____.

3. _____.

4. _____.

5. _____.

6. _____.

7. _____.

8. _____.

9. _____.

10. _____.

A. I'm really worried about your heart.

B. Really, Doctor?
Should I stop eating rich desserts?

A. Mr. Jones!   You MUST stop eating rich desserts!
If you don't stop eating rich desserts, you're going to have serious
problems with your heart some day.

A. I'm really worried about your _____.

B. Really, Doctor?
Should I _____?

A. (Mr./Miss/Mrs./Ms.) _____!   You MUST _____!
If you don't _____, you're going to have serious
problems with your _____ some day.

1. *lungs*
stop smoking

2. *liver*
stop drinking liquor

3. *blood pressure*
take life a little easier

4. *back*
start doing exercises

5. *ears*
stop listening to loud
rock music

6.

HOME REMEDIES

What do YOU do when you burn your finger?

 Some people rub butter on their finger.

 Other people put a piece of ice on their finger.

 Other people put their finger under cold water.

Different people have different remedies for medical problems that aren't very serious. The people below need your advice. Help them with their medical problems and share your "home remedies" with the other students in your class.

1.
   I have a cold. What should I do?

2.
   I have a stomachache. What should I do?

3.
   I have a toothache. What should I do?

4.
   I have a bloody nose. What should I do?

5.
   I have the hiccups. What should I do?

Future Continuous Tense

I	will	I'll		
He	will	He'll		
She	will	She'll		
It	will →	It'll	}	be working.
We	will	We'll		
You	will	You'll		
They	will	They'll		

A. Will you be home this evening?

B. Yes, I will. I'll be reading.

1. *Sharon*

2. *Steven*

3. *Mr. and Mrs. Williams*

4. *Bob*

5. *you*

6. *Kathy*

7. *Jack*

8. *you*

9. *Mrs. McDonald*

10. *you and your brother*

11. *Dave*

12. *you*

Read and practice.

A. Hi, Gloria. This is Arthur.
Can I come over and visit this evening?

B. No, Arthur. I'm afraid I won't be home this evening. I'll be shopping at the supermarket.

A. Can I come over and visit TOMORROW evening?

B. No, Arthur. I'm afraid I won't be home tomorrow evening. I'll be working late at the office.

A. Can I come over and visit this WEEKEND?

B. No, Arthur. I'll be visiting my sister in New York.

A. Can I come over and visit next Wednesday?

B. No, Arthur. I'll be visiting my uncle in the hospital.

A. How about some time next SPRING?

B. No, Arthur. I'll be getting married next spring.

A. Oh!

B. Good-bye.

Complete this conversation.

I'm having some problems with the homework for tomorrow.

I'll be glad to help.
When can you come over?

I can come over at _____ o'clock.
Is that O.K.?

I'm afraid I won't be home at _____ o'clock.
I'll be _____ing. How about _____ o'clock?

No, I won't be able to come over at _____ o'clock.
I'll be _____ing. How about _____ o'clock?

Fine. I'll see you then.

A. How long will your Aunt Gertrude be staying with us?

B. She'll be staying with us **for a few months.**

1. How long will they be staying in San Francisco?
until Friday

3. How late will your husband be working tonight?
until 10 o'clock

5. How much longer will you be practicing the piano?
for a few more minutes

7. When will we be arriving in London?
at 7 a.m.

9. How far will we be driving today?
until we reach Detroit

2. How much longer will you be working on my car?
for a few more hours

4. Where will you be getting off?
at the last stop

6. How late will your daughter be studying English this evening?
until 8 o'clock

8. How much longer will you be reading?
until I finish this chapter

10. How soon will Santa Claus be coming?
in a few days

Read and practice.

A. Hello, Richard.   This is Julie.
I want to return the tennis racket I borrowed from you last week.
Will you be home today at about five o'clock?

B. Yes, I will.   I'll be cooking dinner.

A. Oh, well.   Then I won't come over at five.

B. Why not?

A. I don't want to disturb you.   You'll be cooking dinner!

B. Don't worry.   You won't disturb me.

A. O.K.   I'll see you at five.

A. Hello, _____. This is _____.
I want to return the _____ I borrowed from you last week.
Will you be home today at about _____ o'clock?

B. Yes, I will. I'll be _____ing.

A. Oh, well. Then I won't come over at _____.

B. Why not?

A. I don't want to disturb you. You'll be _____ing!

B. Don't worry. You won't disturb me.

A. O.K. I'll see you at _____.

1. *book*
doing the laundry

2. *record*
watching my favorite TV program

3. *hammer*
helping my son with his homework

4. *coffee pot*
knitting

5. *football*
ironing

6.

30

**Some/Any
Pronoun Review
Verb Tense Review**

I	me	my	mine	myself
you	you	your	yours	yourself
he	him	his	his	himself
she	her	her	hers	herself
it	it	its	its	itself
we	us	our	ours	ourselves
you	you	your	yours	yourselves
they	them	their	theirs	themselves

A. What's **Johnny** doing?

B. **He's** getting dressed.

A. Does **he** need any help?
I'll be glad to help **him**.

B. No, that's O.K.
He can get dressed by **himself**.

1. *your husband*
   fix the TV

2. *your daughter*
   feed the canary

3. *your children*
   cook breakfast

4. *you and your husband*
   clean the garage

5. *your sister*
   fix her car

6. *your son*
   take out the garbage

7. *Bobby and Billy*
   clean their bedroom

8. *you*
   do my homework

9.

190

A. I just found this watch. Is it yours?

B. No, it isn't mine. But it might be **Fred's**.
He lost **his** a few days ago.

A. Thanks. I'll call **him** right away.

1. *umbrella*
Susan's

2. *briefcase*
John's

3. *pocketbook*
Maria's

4. *wallet*
George's

5. *camera*
Mr. and Mrs. Green's

6. *notebook*
Margaret's

7. *ring*
Albert's

8. *transistor radio*
Bobby and Billy's

9. *address book*
Edward's

10. *sneakers*
Helen's

11. *glasses*
Elizabeth's

12.

A. You look tired today.

B. Yes, I know. I couldn't fall asleep last night.

A. Why not?

B. My **neighbors** were **arguing**.

A. How late did they **argue**?

B. They **argued** until 3 a.m.

A. That's terrible! Did you call and complain?

B. No, I didn't. I don't like to complain.

A. Well, I hope you sleep better tonight.

B. I'm sure I will. My **neighbors** don't **argue** very often.

1. *neighbor's son*
   practice the violin

2. *neighbor's dog*
   bark

3. *neighbor's daughter*
listen to her stereo

4. *upstairs neighbors*
play cards

5. *downstairs neighbors*
dance

6. *neighbor across the hall*
sing

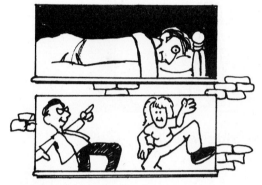

7. *next door neighbors*
clean their apartment

8. *neighbor's daughter*
play the piano

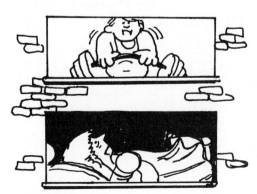

9. *neighbor's son*
lift weights

10.

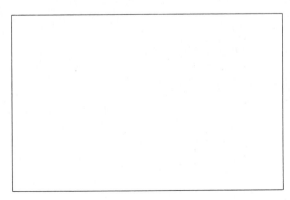

something	anything
{ somebody } { someone }	{ anybody } { anyone }

A. There's something wrong with my **washing machine**.

B. I'm sorry. I can't help you.
I don't know ANYTHING about **washing machines**.

A. Do you know anybody who can help me?

B. Not really. You should look in the phone book.*
I'm sure you'll find somebody who can fix your **washing machine**.

*You can also say, "in the yellow pages." Businesses are listed in the yellow pages of the telephone book.

1. *stove*

2. *TV*

3. *refrigerator*

4. *kitchen sink*

5. *bathtub*

6. *dishwasher*

7. *piano*

8. *radiator*

9.

Read and practice this conversation.

A. Hello. May I please speak to Mr. Armstrong?

B. This is Mr. Armstrong. Can I help you?

A. Yes. There's something wrong with my kitchen sink and I need a good plumber who can come over and fix it as soon as possible.

B. Where do you live?

A. I live at 156 Grove Street in Centerville.

B. I can come over tomorrow at four o'clock. Is that O.K.?

A. Not really. I'm afraid I won't be home tomorrow at four o'clock. I'll be taking my son to the dentist. Can you come at any other time?

B. Not this week. I'm really busy.
I won't be able to come over until some time next week.

A. That's too late. I guess I'll have to call somebody else.
Thank you anyway.

B. Good-bye.

A. Good-bye.

A. Hello. May I please speak to (Mr./Mrs./Miss/Ms.) _____?

B. This is (Mr./Mrs./Miss/Ms.) _____. Can I help you?

A. Yes. There's something wrong with my _____ and I need a good _____ who can come over and fix it as soon as possible.

B. Where do you live?

A. I live at _____ in _____.

B. I can come over tomorrow at _____ o'clock. Is that O.K.?

A. Not really. I'm afraid I won't be home tomorrow at _____ o'clock. I'll be _____ing. Can you come at any other time?

B. Not this week. I'm really busy. I won't be able to come over until some time next week.

A. That's too late. I guess I'll have to call somebody else. Thank you anyway.

B. Good-bye.

A. Good-bye.

1. *electrician*

2. *TV repairman*

3. *piano tuner*

4. *plumber*

5.

APPENDIX

**Cardinal Numbers
Ordinal Numbers
Irregular Verbs:
Past Tense**

Cardinal Numbers

1	one	13	thirteen
2	two	14	fourteen
3	three	15	fifteen
4	four	16	sixteen
5	five	17	seventeen
6	six	18	eighteen
7	seven	19	nineteen
8	eight		
9	nine		
10	ten		
11	eleven		
12	twelve		

20	twenty
21	twenty-one
22	twenty-two
.	.
.	.
29	twenty-nine
30	thirty
40	forty
50	fifty
60	sixty
70	seventy
80	eighty
90	ninety

100	one hundred
200	two hundred
300	three hundred
.	.
.	.
.	.
900	nine hundred

1,000	one thousand
2,000	two thousand
3,000	three thousand
.	.
.	.
10,000	ten thousand
100,000	one hundred thousand
1,000,000	one million

Ordinal Numbers

1st	first	13th	thirteenth	20th	twentieth
2nd	second	14th	fourteenth	21st	twenty-first
3rd	third	15th	fifteenth	22nd	twenty-second
4th	fourth	16th	sixteenth	.	.
5th	fifth	17th	seventeenth	.	.
6th	sixth	18th	eighteenth	29th	twenty-ninth
7th	seventh	19th	nineteenth	30th	thirtieth
8th	eighth			40th	fortieth
9th	ninth			50th	fiftieth
10th	tenth			60th	sixtieth
11th	eleventh			70th	seventieth
12th	twelfth			80th	eightieth
				90th	ninetieth

one hundredth

one thousandth

one millionth

How to read a date:

June 9, 1941 = "June ninth, nineteen forty-one"

Irregular Verbs: Past Tense

be	was	light	lit
begin	began	lose	lost
bite	bit	make	made
break	broke	meet	met
bring	brought	put	put
buy	bought	read	read
catch	caught	ride	rode
come	came	run	ran
cut	cut	say	said
do	did	see	saw
drink	drank	sell	sold
drive	drove	send	sent
eat	ate	shake	shook
fall	fell	sing	sang
feed	fed	sit	sat
feel	felt	sleep	slept
fight	fought	speak	spoke
find	found	stand	stood
fly	flew	steal	stole
forget	forgot	sweep	swept
get	got	swim	swam
give	gave	take	took
go	went	teach	taught
grow	grew	tell	told
have	had	think	thought
hear	heard	throw	threw
hurt	hurt	understand	understood
know	knew	wear	wore
lead	led	write	wrote
leave	left		

Index